Mums Chat

in the stress and the mess and the
everyone else knows best...

...a biblical boost for your faith, hope and love

Marianne Fernandez

Sarah
GRACE
PUBLISHING
Dyslexic Friendly

Based on the globally enjoyed *Mums Chat* video collection hosted by RightNow Media. Shining God's comfort and truth plus some down-to-earth humour into your early-years parenting struggles.

Look who's talking about *Mums Chat* . . .

"*Mums Chat is such a great read. I loved the song element as music can be so uplifting and can definitely affect emotions. I liked the fact that the font size is bigger for tired eyes. I remember feeling soo very tired.*"

Rachel Humphries - mum to Andrew and Jonathan, UK

"*Your words are kind and truly uplifting to this mama. So many aspects of our lives can make us feel lonely and isolated, and yet whenever I listen to you it seems as though I'm talking to someone I've always been friends with. It is wonderful to know we are not alone . . . and that there is a very real and powerful God fighting for us.*"

Meshel Bussey, minister's wife and mom, USA

"*Marianne has dedicated herself to addressing some of the most sensitive parenting taboos within both society and the church. We are pleased to partner with Marianne and OptiMums. Her compassion for others and her love of God shine.*"

RightNow Media, USA

"*I have watched your* Mums Chat *collection twice. I really like your goal, as a mother, to help families where there are wounds that need to be healed. I send blessings from the Lord.*"

Ignasi Ricart I Fabregas, Doctor of Theology
Claretian Missionaries (1948–2021), Spain

First published 2023 by Sarah Grace Publishing,
an imprint of Malcolm Down Publishing Ltd
www.malcolmdown.co.uk

27 26 25 24 23   7 6 5 4 3 2 1

British Library Cataloguing in Publication Data
A catalogue record for this book is available from the British Library.

ISBN: 978-1-915046-66-6

Cover design by Lush Creative
Typesetting by Angela Selfe

Printed in the UK

This book is for
Ania
&
Daniel

The Mums Chat Mission

The *Mums Chat* collection calms and restores
Uplifts your spirit among the chores.
From dreams of motherhood to starting school
Life can be tough and life can be cruel.
The *Mums Chat* mission for mums worldwide:
"You are not alone, I AM by your side.
In the waiting and hoping and barely coping.
In the stress and the mess and the everyone-else-knows-best.
Come sit a while, come listen, come see
Let Mums Chat *bring you closer to Me."*

Contents

Marianne's Backstory   9
How To Get The Most From This Book   17
How To Make This Book Your Own   21

Infant Section   23
    Parental Responsibility   25
    Postnatal Depression   34
    Sleep Deprivation   50
    Body Image   60

Bouncing Baby Section   73
    Baby Milestones and Competitive Mothers 75
    Lost Identity   85
    Teething   94
    Guilty Mother Syndrome   103

Toddler Section   113
    Starting Childcare   116
    Baby Brain   126
    Small Children and Church   139
    When Patience Runs Out   152

Starting School Section   161
    Toilet Training, Buttons and Zips   164
    Staying In The Present Moment   179
    First Day At School   192

Author's Comments   203
Acknowledgments   207

Marianne's Backstory

Hello,

Would you like to know my backstory? Personally, I like to get a feel for a writer before reading their book, but a normal author's biography is quite short and usually leaves me wanting more. It's not so much that I want them to dig the dirt or give me the gossip; it's about connecting and finding unexpected common ground, so I feel like I know them better as a person before I start reading.

So, this author's bio is a bit longer because, if I'd never met me before, this is what I'd want to know. I've written it as if you were interviewing me. It's a quick walk through my background, what shaped me, just how wobbly my faith walk has been and what brought me to write Mums Chat. Alternatively, if you're a dive-straight-in girl with no FOMO, then feel free to skip this bit.

Where did it all start?

I was born in Wrexham, Wales, to loving but far-from-affluent parents. Dad is from the north-east of England, Mum is from the Welsh valleys. Both knew significant hardship before they met, and both knew that education

and qualifications would get them a better future –
eventually. But financial security took a while to achieve and

"Put it back! We can't afford it"

are the words I most associate with my early childhood.
My mum made sure we never went hungry, but money
was tight and pass-me-down clothes were gratefully
received from family and friends. As a little girl I remember
watching my dad study in the evenings for his engineering
degree. I'd sit next to him after he came home from work
and I'd scribble as I did my "homework" too. These early
memories were my motivation to succeed at school, to get
a degree of my own and a self-supporting career.

What about your faith? You haven't mentioned that yet.

My mum is a practising Christian and, again from my
earliest memories, I recall that she always went to church
and took me and my little sister too. As Dad's career
gathered pace we moved around the country and Mum
took me to many different places of worship. I came to see
that God is at work in every part of His church. As a child
I went to the Church of Wales followed by an evangelical
home church and, much later on, after my spectacularly
backslidden twenties, I went to a Methodist church for a
short while. I worshipped for a long period in a Catholic
church and during the Covid lockdowns I attended various
churches online. Now I'm going to an evangelical church
in Swindon. It's based in an historic railway building
and is very family friendly. It even has a twisty slide
inside the building, so the younger kids can slide down
from reception to join the church service. So, in terms
of my faith, I have quite a blended background and I'm

comfortable worshipping in a wide variety of places. I feel non-denominational, which means I don't have a Christian "brand" I feel I have to stick to. The one common factor is that whatever church I've called "mine" – Jesus has always been there to meet me.

What do you mean when you say, "spectacularly backslidden twenties"?

Oh yes, I thought you'd ask about that. Well, I was spurred on by a deep-seated need for financial independence. I got my degree and found work afterwards in a succession of global corporations. Finally, I had the career I'd always dreamed of. I travelled to many far-flung places on business trips. I managed large teams and large budgets. I lived with the endless emails and meetings. For me, corporate life was all-consuming and I was willing to let it take over. I became a selfish, proud workaholic, totally controlled and defined by my job. I decided I could manage my life just fine on my own thanks. I regularly worked 10 hours and more a day and I stopped going to church. I didn't need faith, just hard work and the next promotion. I thought my need for love could be entirely met by the man in my life at that time. That was my backsliding. I prioritised my career, money and my romantic relationships. I shelved my faith completely.

Why didn't that work for you?

Outwardly I was a success. I had my own home (it was tiny, but I loved it) and a new company car. I was financially self-sufficient. But my personal life was a mess. A good family, a good education and a good job doesn't necessarily give you self-worth. I made poor choices about men throughout my twenties, and I got very hurt. It was after an especially damaging and toxic relationship ended that I crawled in bits prayerfully and tearfully back to God. I realised doing life my way wasn't working for me. Jesus met me in the mess. He picked me up and started a deep inner-healing process that eventually led me to my Spanish husband, Albert.

Ok, so tell me, how did you meet Albert? Was it a holiday romance?

No, not quite! After a period of being single and investing time in myself and my faith walk, I started salsa dancing classes in the lovely Victorian Old Town of Swindon. They were held in an upstairs room of a pub called The Kings Arms and were my weekly escape from work. Dad thought it was a very odd pastime. As a true northern lad, he didn't quite get the appeal of parading around a dancefloor all elbows and hip swivels.

"It's always when you're not looking for someone special . . . that you find The One" a close friend told me at the time.

And I really wasn't looking, I was busy drawing closer to God, starting to see myself as God saw me, learning to forgive myself, value myself and embrace His healing. But Albert quite literally swept me off my feet at my salsa class. Not so tall but certainly dark and very handsome; he was also a churchgoer. By this time, I was in my thirties and in no mood to compromise. I had decided I was only going to date a Christian man with a view to getting married and having a family. Full stop. Albert was similarly minded, and we tied the knot in beautiful Barcelona and settled in a mainly wet village in Wiltshire. Within 5 months of becoming Mr and Mrs, I was pregnant.

So how did you come to write Mums Chat*?*

This book and the *Mums Chat* video series are the by-product of the years that followed. I quickly discovered that becoming a parent was the toughest assignment I'd ever been given. There were moments of joy, obviously, and my daughter was not a difficult baby, but I found it so hard. Undiagnosed postnatal depression meant I'd never felt so alone, out of control of my time, out of my depth in experience, tired, irritable, frumpy and deeply low. I knew I needed to lean on Jesus more than ever, but the first 12 months of being a mum was a very dark time. I really struggled.

Back then I didn't find a down-to-earth guidebook for Christian mums that I could grab that took each of the early-years challenges I was facing and pointed me to where in the Bible I could get help. I wanted to actively use my faith as a support during this time, but I needed help to do that, and my attempts were hit and miss.

I didn't have a young mum Christian friend at my church who could be a role model and get alongside me and uplift me and tell me that I was actually doing a great job as a parent and reassure me that all would be well when, for all my praying, I didn't feel Jesus by my side. I just felt alone.

Why did you feel alone? You had Albert, right?

It was lonely partly because I didn't have any family living nearby to support me but also because this phase of life coincided with Albert being away Monday to Friday working in Madrid. I think I understand a bit of how military wives must feel. When I was on my own, I had to find a way to juggle work and parenting by myself. I'd get into a finely tuned routine. Then Albert would come home and it took time to adjust. Then just as I got used to him being around, he'd go again.

Eventually, we were blessed to have two children, but the journey was far from easy. A miscarriage and several years of unexplained secondary infertility were deep, dark valleys that I've shared very openly in *Mums Chat* videos to provide Bible-based support and comfort to others in their loss.

So, Mums Chat *started as a video series and now it's a book. Is it the book you wish you'd had?*

Yes, it is definitely the resource I wish I'd had. I think the *Mums Chat* video collection lends itself well to becoming a book because, despite our TikTok video culture, people do still want to sit down quietly and read something. There's a sense of peace in reading at your own pace without constant pop-ups and alerts vying for your attention.

The topics in this book are really tricky when you are going through them. And when numerous challenges hit at the same time, which they often do, it's even harder. In the midst of all this to have a voice of positivity, an uplifting word, another person to say:

> *"Yes, actually this is difficult, but you are doing really well and you will get through this"*

is so valuable. So, basically, this is the book I wish I'd had. It's the down-to-earth, Christian guidebook for mums that I wanted to grab, addressing each of the early-years challenges I was facing. It's the book that hopefully makes others smile in recognition of "Oh yeah! I do that!" I'm certainly not a saint and the stories I share in these pages lay bare my parenting and spiritual shortcomings. But God still loves me and I hope that comes across too.

Where do we go if we want to know more?

The best place I can direct you to go is my company website www.optimums.co.uk. When I became a parent, I quickly discovered I was unable to fit my corporate job into the suddenly reduced hours I had available. Daily, lengthy overtime was no longer an option as Ania needed collecting from nursery and all my attention when we got home. Equally, I was unwilling to be consumed by the demands of corporate life in the way I had been before. There was a huge imbalance for me, which I really struggled with. After a lot of soul searching, private tears and prayers I faced the fact that my life had changed and my career needed to change too.

So, I left the corporate world to retrain as a coach and set up OptiMums. I now provide maternity coaching for mums returning to work after maternity leave and I also offer executive coaching for women and men seeking help to maximise their sense of fulfilment in their career. Oh, and I've written the *Mums Chat* collection and this book too.

When you visit my website, you can click the tab called The Story So Far which gives a very open account of my God-led career and explains how the *Mums Chat* pilot video for RightNow Media came about. The website also enables you to watch the free Intro videos for the *Mums Chat* collection and gives me the chance to say a personal, "Hello and welcome!"

How To Get The Most From This Book

Mums Chat was created to help us mums draw closer to God as we care for our little ones. A resource to bolster us during the nappy changing, sleep deprivation, milk feeds, laundry and endless mess. Something to help as our babies grow and new challenges appear.

I'm aware that a wide variety of women (and possibly men) might read this book. We are united in each being a parent, but we are all individuals with different family units. Some of us are married, some of us have a partner, some of us are single parents. Some of us feel we have a mature faith whilst others of us would describe our faith as in the budding early stages. Some of us might not claim to have any faith at all and are just curious to know how it might make a difference. Some of us have just had our first baby and others are juggling meeting the needs of more than one small person. Some of us have a robust network of local support whilst others of us feel we really are alone and without help (sometimes you can feel alone even when there is another adult in the house).

In order to make the content more applicable and better meet your needs I've included three different elements after each of the 15 topics:

1) Putting it into practice

Firstly, I've included a section to help make more sense of the spiritual. Sometimes the "putting it into practice" bit is at the end of a topic and sometimes it's within the main body of a topic, depending on what flows best.

Every mum reading this book will be at a different point with her faith. For those who were born and raised in a Christian family and are actively attending church then turning Bible verses into actions might be second nature. But for mums whose faith walk is in its early stages or who don't go to church or who stopped going or have never been, then making this Bible stuff work in real life might not be so obvious or straight forward.

For some of you these suggestions might reaffirm what you are already doing or be something you hadn't considered and would like to try. Alternatively, these options might spark an idea of your own as to how you could activate your faith your way. Whatever works for you – go for it! If you are drawing near to God, then He will draw near to you.

2) Practical pomp-free prayers

Secondly, I've added a short prayer at the end of each topic. They are written as I would pray them so not in a traditional church style. My prayers are my conversations with God and I don't need to put on airs and graces for Him.

For those of you who have a more developed faith these prayers might not be needed because you are quite used to forming your own. For those whose faith is still in its early stages then it can feel a bit weird to pray and hear your voice saying words you might not normally say like, "Hello God, it's me here . . ."

So, I've included the prayers for those who want to get started with a prayer life and also for those who would like a little extra help maybe due to sleep deprivation. It's basically talking to God or Jesus the way you would talk to a trusted friend and remembering to expect a reply (we'll cover the reply bit in more detail later).

3) A song chosen just for you

Finally, I've added a contemporary Christian song recommendation at the end of each topic. Please note that none of the artists I've mentioned endorse *Mums Chat* (yet) but their songs add an extra dimension of support. I've chosen each song carefully to speak into that particular struggle through the lyrics, to uplift you and help you to praise and worship your way through to the other side. Praise and worship songs are not limited to traditional hymns. If the lyrics are faith filled and God focused – it's praise and worship and its powerful to strengthening your faith and finding a winning way through the woe.

It might come as a surprise to you that Christian music exists in every genre you can imagine. The most obvious are choral and gospel music, but nowadays even heavy metal, hip-hop, reggae and rock have Christian groups. All the songs I'm recommending are by modern contemporary artists who post video and / or lyric versions of their songs on YouTube and elsewhere so you should be able to stream them easily. I recommend the official lyric versions so you can read the words, but just enjoy them however works best for you. I chose them with you in mind knowing they have helped me in the past.

Whilst I'm not a music journalist I've tried to explain, in my own way, what makes them special. Do make time to listen to them. They are just as important as the words in this book and, used together, combine into a very powerful response to the challenge you are facing. Try it. You'll see what I mean.

How To Make This Book Your Own

Each person's faith walk is individual. I can't have your faith walk and you can't have mine. We each need to find, nurture and grow our friendship with Jesus our own way and in our own time. Your conversations with Him are special because they are as unique as you are.

Please see this book as opening a door to using your faith to connect practically with your Creator Father God, with your Saviour Jesus Christ and with the Giver of life, the Holy Spirit.

Please let this book reassure you that hours of prayer and Bible study are thankfully not necessary to grow your faith in this season. Sometimes you might find you do have the time and energy to have a short prayer time and quiet read of your Bible, and that's great – well done! Most days you probably won't, so don't beat yourself up.

I find Jesus waiting for me in my regular short prayers throughout the day – my prayers for help, to say thank you, to ask for patience, for wisdom or even a parking space in town. This is how a great many Christian mums maintain and grow their relationship with Jesus in their baby's early years. It's an on-the-run kind of prayer life. It's a grab-it-and-keep-going kind of Bible reading time. It's a "Holy Spirit, please fill-me-up-with-Your-power-now-because-I-will-forget-to-ask-You-later, Amen" sort of spiritual topping-up process.

This book reflects that season. It is something quick and to the point. Each topic is purposefully short in length for those who don't have much time. Printed in big font for tired eyes. Something to pick up and put down as time allows.

Finally, this book says:

- please scribble in my margins,
- use your colourful highlighter pens at will,
- feel free to fold my corners down,
- make me look well-thumbed and
- enjoy filling the "Mum Memories" personal journalling sections. This is your blank space to use as you choose.

This book is the result of my own laughter and tears. I have not spared my blushes. It's all there. My God, my babies and me. I pray that you will unlock spiritual truth, peace, hope and strength from within these pages for your own parenting journey.

Blessings on you and your little one(s),

Marianne x

Infant Section

Welcome to the Infant section. From the moment our little ones are born our lives are forever changed. Having birthed these tiny beings into the world they occupy every moment day and night in this season. The Infant section covers some of the universal challenges that parents of a newborn can face. Each topic is "a biggy" but sometimes these challenges can come all at once.

It's no wonder it can be a 24/7 struggle. But we don't need to struggle alone. Each section below helps you to take your situation to Jesus and seek His comfort, rest and reassurance. I share my own dark days in order to brighten yours, and I pray you come through this season knowing both you and your precious little one are held by Him.

Here are the topics covered and the recommended songs (three by Francesca Battistelli in this section – I'm a big fan):

Parental Responsibility

    Recommended song

    "Run To Jesus" by Francesca Battistelli

Postnatal Depression

> Recommended song
> "If We're Honest" by Francesca Battistelli

Sleep Deprivation

> Recommended song
> "Find Rest" by Francesca Battistelli

Body Image

> Recommended song
> "True Beauty" by Mandisa

Finally, if you would like to "meet" me before you read this section then feel free to watch my short, friendly, Infant Series Intro video.

Just scan the QR code or, if you are reading an eBook, follow the infant-series link. It will take you to the courses part of my website at www.optimums.co.uk and from there to a very nice kitchen.

Here's the link:

https://mumschat.thinkific.com/courses/infant-series

Here's the QR code

Parental Responsibility

What exactly do I mean by parental responsibility? Well, I'm referring to that moment, whenever it comes, that you find yourself alone for the first time without any support from hospital staff or family members after the birth of your child. The weight of responsibility sits squarely on your shoulders and you feel out of your depth.

This moment arrives at different times for each of us. I had an extended stay in hospital after the birth of my daughter and I was able to access a unit that gave extra support to learn breastfeeding. The midwives running the unit were so caring. On my first night they offered to take my baby away for a few hours so that I could sleep. I was so relieved not to be expected to look after my daughter on my own immediately after giving birth. I was exhausted, sore from stitches, still bleeding and my uterus was still contracting painfully at regular intervals.

The midwife team were baby experts and I gladly trusted them to help me and my daughter. A few days later when I went home, my mum was there to help for a couple of weeks. She is a Christian, a trained nurse and obviously a mum herself so her presence was very reassuring for me and my husband.

But the moment came when my husband went back to work and my mum drove herself back to Wales, about 3 hours away. I remember very well standing in the country lane outside my home and waving her, my safety net, goodbye. I felt lost, incapable, totally out of my depth and I cried as I walked back into my house to face being the primary carer to my daughter on my own for the first time. It felt very lonely and the weight of responsibility rested so heavily on my new-mum shoulders.

Even though I knew I had to "dig deep", "roll up my sleeves" and "get on with it" it took me a long time to feel ready to leave the house on my own with my daughter. I was worried about my ability to care for her, about her getting a virus, about my ability to lift her big pram in and out of the car, about what I'd do if she needed a nappy change or breastfeeding while we were out.

I hadn't come to terms with life now being messy and unpredictable with baby bodily functions spilling out at random intervals. I needed reassurance in bucket loads. I'd given birth on a beautiful day in July and the summer weather was glorious. I could have been outside enjoying the fresh air with my daughter but I spent at least another week mainly inside recovering from childbirth and gaining my confidence to leave the house. When I did finally venture out my baby bag was packed ready for every conceivable situation – it was HUGE!

For a new mum encouragement and reassurance that you are doing just fine is a necessity in those early days. Finding your feet as a parent, especially once you are on your own with sole responsibility for your baby, takes time. You need wisdom that you don't have and confidence that you don't feel.

Let's take a look at a similar situation from the Old Testament. Solomon felt very much like this when he was suddenly made King of Israel by his bedridden father King

David, just before his death. Solomon was not expected to become king. He was not David's oldest son. But God told David that Solomon should be his successor and suddenly Solomon was responsible for an entire nation's wellbeing and leadership. He had not received kingly training. His elder brother Adonijah would have been the natural choice to receive that and all the Israelites expected the oldest son to become king. Just imagine if, following the death of Queen Elizabeth II in the UK, Prince Edward had suddenly been announced as king instead of his elder brother Charles. It would be a similar situation. Goodness gracious! How shocking!

But Adonijah displeased God and he was passed over. Solomon was thrust into the limelight with not only kingly responsibility but the job of building God's temple in Jerusalem. Oh, how Solomon must have felt like a new mum with her first infant when he became leader of the Israelites. And now that his father was dead who could he turn to for help? His safety net was gone.

We know that responsibility landed heavily on his shoulders because Solomon prayed in 1 Kings 3:7-9 (AMP) saying:

> Now, O Lord my God, You have made Your servant king in place of David, my father, and I am but a lad [in wisdom and experience]; I know not how to go out (begin) or come in (finish). Your servant is in the midst of Your people whom You have chosen, a great people who cannot be counted for multitude. So give Your servant an understanding mind and a hearing heart to judge Your people, that I may discern between good and bad. For who is able to judge and rule this Your great people?

Solomon knew he was totally out of his depth. He felt like a boy doing a man's job, inadequate and ill prepared. King Solomon asked for wisdom and God was pleased and granted his request. In the same way – if you feel inadequate and ill prepared God will certainly answer your prayer for parental wisdom in raising your child.

James 1:5 (NIV) confirms this:

> If any of you lacks wisdom, you should ask God, who gives generously to all without finding fault, and it will be given to you.

Please be reassured – this feeling of being out of your depth with your parental responsibilities is universal. Every first-time parent and many second and third-time-plus parents feel the same, but God has wisdom available to us if we choose to ask Him for it. And we will need it not only when our children are tiny babies but throughout parenthood. Every stage of raising a child throws up new challenges that we will navigate so much more skilfully with God's wisdom.

Matthew 7:7 (NIV) says:

> Ask and it will be given to you; seek and you will find.

So let your heart be reassured. You will have to learn by doing, like every parent before you, and also like Solomon, but you have access to God's wisdom to help you, and with God's wisdom comes God's peace.

Colossians 3:15 (GNT) tells us:

> The peace that Christ gives is to guide you in the decisions you make.

Putting it into practice

The three points below certainly helped me. I hope they help you too.

1) Taking time out

For me praying for wisdom was also twinned with taking some time out to stop. When I felt overwhelmed, I would breathe in and out deeply for a little while so I could find my feet. I would focus my thoughts on the Bible verses above. I would say calmly out loud that I trust God's Word to be true. I believe His promises to me are real. Then I would pray for God's wisdom and peace to come into my head and my heart as I got on with my parental responsibilities. It was never a long prayer, my in-the-moment prayers rarely are.

2) Listening for that small voice of calm

Then afterwards I would make the house quiet and try to hear that small, reassuring voice of calm in my mind telling me to slow down. Telling me I was doing just fine. Guiding me through the minutia of my day, one chore at a time. If you ask Him, God will help you. If you take a little time to listen, He will show you. God imparts His wisdom to us in an infinite variety of ways after we have asked for it.

3) Being open to how wisdom comes in answer to prayer

Keep your ears and eyes open. You might get the reassurance you need through a random radio interview or a book or magazine. It could be that you gain a valuable insight that helps you through a TV programme. Perhaps a friend opens up about their own struggle and how they coped, and it shines a light for you onto your situation. Maybe a blog hits the spot.

For some of us the input we are getting from whatever source, be it family, friends, social media or wherever, might actually be doing more harm than good to confidence levels. Wisdom might prompt you to assess if the inputs you have been using for support perhaps need trimming back or deprioritising.

God can answer your prayers for parental wisdom in a myriad of ways. It is unlikely that you will find two Moses-like tablets of stone engraved with 10 instructions at the bottom of your bed every morning. But if you will pray and then start to become tuned in and open to the ways God uses to reach you, you will find Him reaching out to help you.

For most Christians God uses His Word to speak to us, so if you have a Bible just open it anywhere and see what He shows you. If you don't have a Bible maybe you can buy or borrow one. Getting your hands on a physical Bible that you actually open and actually read is the best way to hear from Him. If Bible reading is very new to you then maybe start by looking up the verses mentioned in this book and see what else your eye is drawn to. You might have heard the National Lottery phrase:

"You have to be in it to win it!"

Well, obviously I don't recommend gambling but when it comes to the Bible something similar applies:

"You have to read to feed!"

God will meet you where you are and give you new ideas, maybe lead you to new information, perhaps provide you with feedback or open opportunities to try new things that will be beneficial.

Be blessed, reassured and steadied. God's wisdom will surely find you.

 Prayer

Heavenly Father,

Thank You for Your Bible that contains so many promises of help for me. Thank You that Your words are true, and I can rely on them.

There are times when being a parent is overwhelming. I'm expected to know everything straight away and I really do want to do a good job, but I lack experience and confidence because this is all so new. I just get to grips with one stage and then another unfolds and I feel like I'm starting again.

Your Word says that You promise to give me wisdom if I ask for it, so, heavenly Father, I am here asking. As I learn on the job, please help me to feel calm and slowed and reassured that You are with me every step I take.

Give me ears and eyes to recognise the help You are sending to me. Help me to receive the parental wisdom I've asked for and put it into practice. Thank You, Father.

In Jesus' name I ask,

Amen

Recommended song

"Run To Jesus" by Francesca Battistelli

Written by: Francesca Battistelli, Ben Glover, Jennifer Schott, David Garcia

Francesca Battistelli is a world-famous contemporary Christian singer, songwriter and performer. She is a Grammy Award winner and has millions of followers on social media. Her voice is clear and strong, and the melodies in her work vary considerably song to song. She is the mother of a large young family and, as a result, much of her work seems, to me, to be written from a mother's perspective. I guess this is why her songs feature frequently in this book. Francesca has been a blessing to me and I am so glad to recommend her work.

I chose this song for you because the title suggests exactly what I wanted to do when my husband went back to work and my mum drove away and left me, on that sunny July morning, on my own with my tiny baby. I just wanted to run to someone for help. The lyrics speak of being bewildered and lost, which is exactly how I felt. Overwhelmed and out of my depth. It's a loud, high-tempo track with lots of drums. It's an upbeat song and I can imagine myself running towards Jesus when I listen to the chorus. There's no shame or failure in needing help. He's waiting for you.

Mum Memories

Your space to use as you choose.

Suggestion

What ways and which people do you think God might use to reach you and answer your prayer? What/who has reassured, encouraged or uplifted you recently?

Postnatal Depression

This is one subject that, in my experience, is not usually a topic of conversation at mother and baby groups. I believe postnatal depression affects far more women than are ever diagnosed by a doctor. This is because, for whatever reason, many mums are still reluctant to talk to others and ask for help. Postnatal depression simply doesn't fit with the perfect social media life so many portray.

I know this because I was one of those mums. I battled this illness alone and in silence and I remember very clearly the fear and the pride that made me hide my sadness from everyone. I was afraid of being judged by my family and health professionals.

I was worried that my baby would be taken away if I admitted that I wasn't coping so well. I was too proud to accept that I might be suffering from a mental illness and I was afraid of the stigma that might attach to me if I was diagnosed. I wanted to be seen by everyone as a capable mother. Does this sound familiar?

Let me reassure you that all of my fears and prejudices were unfounded. I have since discussed this topic with both a midwife and a family doctor and they both confirmed that mums with postnatal depression are treated with compassion by health professionals. The focus is on helping mums, not judging them.

Treatment is tailored to the mum depending on whether she is experiencing mild, moderate or severe symptoms.

So, how common is it and what are the symptoms of postnatal depression?

According to the USA government website:[1]

"On average 13% of women have symptoms of depression after the birth of a baby."

We can estimate that, in the USA, this equates to over 460,000 mums every year (based on 3.6 million live births annually as per the CDC website).[2] That sounds like a lot of mums to me.

The picture is similar in the UK where the NHS website[3] states that:

"An estimated 1 in 10 women suffer postnatal depression after giving birth. Interestingly it can affect new fathers too and is more than just feeling low for a few weeks after giving birth, which is commonly called the 'baby blues'. Postnatal depression usually lasts longer, sometimes for months. Symptoms vary but can include:

- Feeling low for a long period of time

- Feeling emotional and tearful

- Tiredness

- Lack of interest in yourself and / or your new baby

- Difficulty sleeping

- Feeling useless, worthless, guilty

1. www.cdc.gov
2. Permission granted by Centers for Disease Control and Prevention (CDC) (page last reviewed May 2, 2022).
   Content source: Division of Reproductive Health, National Center for Chronic Disease Prevention and Health Promotion
3. www.nhs.uk

- Feeling overwhelmed with normal life
- Having unrealistic expectations of motherhood
- Feeling alone
- Feeling loss of control
- Having worrying thoughts about hurting your baby."[4]

Looking back, I am convinced I had postnatal depression when my daughter was born and it was truly awful. I didn't feel like myself at all. I felt unable to cope with normal life. The smallest things took superhuman effort to do and stressed me out and I was afraid of the responsibility of being a mum and the main carer. I questioned everything I did. The house was a mess and I blamed myself for the clutter.

I felt anxious all the time and the accusing voice in my head was relentless. Every waking moment it criticised and belittled everything I did. I've never felt so low or alone. I occasionally had worrying thoughts about hurting my baby, which was truly shocking to me. It took me years to find the courage to share this with someone. I told a trusted friend who had also suffered postnatal depression and she instantly admitted she had experienced something similar. But at the time, out of fear and pride, I didn't talk to anyone about my depression and I sincerely wish I had. Instead, I struggled for months, often sitting alone on my bedroom floor with my head in my hands, crying as negative thoughts came time and again and dark emotions blotted out the joy of having my new baby.

---

4. Permission to quote from NHS website granted via statement:
Contains public sector information licensed under the Open Government Licence v3.0

If you recognise yourself in this place, I urge you please don't suffer in silence like I did. Find someone to talk to. That might be your husband, your partner, a good friend, a family member, your church minister or your doctor. If you prefer to ring a helpline then do that but don't let depression keep you like a prisoner in solitary confinement. I know first-hand that hiding your pain only compounds the suffering. Sharing the truth of your situation really will set you free to start moving forward.

For some mums just having someone to talk to and being given support is enough; for others medical intervention in the form of medication or counselling is effective. This *Mums Chat* offers some powerful biblical resources for you to consider using in place of or alongside whatever other treatment you feel is helpful.

It might surprise you to discover that the Bible has many references to depression within its pages and practical guidance on how to use God's life-giving, uplifting Word effectively. This topic will look at three ways in which postnatal depression attacks us and how the Bible advises us to respond.

The first and second examples are probably most appropriate for mums experiencing mild to moderate postnatal depression symptoms. For mums with more severe symptoms you will probably relate to all three examples.

Attack No 1 – Our Emotions

Firstly, let's look at King David. As a youth David killed Goliath and we imagine he must have been unstoppable, but he suffered depression on a regular basis. However, regardless of how he felt, he was determined to *say* positive God-based truths over himself. He wrote his emotions down as he spoke to his depressed heart in:

Psalm 43:5 (AMP):

> Why are you cast down, O my inner self? And why should you moan over me and be disquieted within me? Hope in God and wait expectantly for Him, for I shall yet praise Him, Who is the help of my [sad] countenance, and my God.

David was determined to *speak to his emotions* and tell them how big God is and how God can overcome anything. What a great example.

David understood that he needed to take a stand against depression no matter how hard it was and he needed to speak his faith out loud "for I shall yet praise Him". You can almost see him forcing the words to come out of his mouth. He was utterly determined to say them despite how dragged down he was feeling in that moment.

Another tactic David used was to tell himself to count his blessings.

Psalm 103:2 (AMP) says:

> Bless (affectionately, gratefully praise) the Lord, O my soul, and forget not [one of] all His benefits.

David knew that there is power in words, especially words of praise and thankfulness. It's as though their power is multiplied when we say them in circumstances when it is especially hard to do so. David spoke God's victory to his depression in the same way that he spoke God's victory to Goliath moments before he defeated him.

If we roll back to 1 Samuel 17:45-47 (AMP):

> David said to the Philistine, You come to me with a sword, a spear, and a javelin, but I come to you in the name of the Lord of hosts, the God of the ranks of Israel, Whom you have defied.

> This day the Lord will deliver you into my hand, and I will smite you and cut off your head . . . that all the earth may know that there is a God in Israel.

> And all this assembly shall know that the Lord saves not with sword and spear; for the battle is the Lord's and He will give you into our hands.

In the same way you can slay the giant called postnatal depression by standing on God's Word, recognising that the battle belongs to the Lord and *speaking* God's Word over your emotions.

 Putting it into practice – Our Emotions

My own days with postnatal depression varied. Some days I had the energy to fight it and on these grey, cloudy days I could clench my fists, grit my teeth and force a Bible-based battle cry out. It didn't necessarily mean that my emotions changed though. Sometimes they did and my mood lifted, yet other times I felt no different afterwards. But I did it anyway, partly because I believed God's promise to help me and partly because of my wider reading on how the brain works.

Psychologists have shown how important our own spoken words are to mental wellbeing. Even if I say these verses and I feel no different immediately afterwards the words go down into what King David calls "my inner self". The words I speak out loud are heard by my subconscious. My subconscious doesn't know my words don't line up with my feelings and it registers the positive, faith-filled utterance of my mouth for my benefit anyway. The Bible was actually way ahead of modern psychology because we find this written in

Proverbs 18:21 (AMP):

Death and life are in the power of the tongue.

So, I chose to use my tongue to bring me slowly back towards the happy, restored life I wanted. I spoke God's Word to my emotions and little by little it helped. It was like each biblical utterance was a brick in a spiritual wall I was building to keep depression at bay. I hope you can do the same, one brick at a time. I didn't always feel an instant release but every brick counts.

Attack No 2 – Our Thoughts

The second example we will look at comes from Paul who shows us that our enemies are not always people. He clearly understood that we can be attacked by *thoughts* when he wrote to the church in Corinth. He told them in

2 Corinthians 10:3-5 (AMP):

For though we walk (live) in the flesh, we are not carrying on our warfare according to the flesh and using mere human weapons.

For the weapons of our warfare are not physical . . . but they are mighty before God for the overthrow and destruction of strongholds [my words i.e. depressive thoughts].

[Inasmuch as we] refute arguments and theories and reasonings and every proud and lofty thing that sets itself up against the [true] knowledge of God; and we lead every thought . . . away captive into the obedience of Christ.

Paul tells us to challenge and manage our *thoughts.* So how do we put this into practice when we live in the real world? How do we conduct warfare in our own head? How do we argue with the voice that tells us we are inadequate and incapable as a mother? How do we lead every negative thought away captive into the obedience of Christ?

I know first-hand that managing thoughts isn't easy, but Paul tells us to challenge and wrestle with them anytime they are out of line with God's view of us. He tells us to get active in weeding out negativity and instead plant positivity. Lead those thoughts away and replace them with scriptures such as Paul wrote in

Romans 8:37 (AMP):

Yet amid all these things we are more than conquerors and gain a surpassing victory through Him.

Well Amen to that but how do we apply it?

Putting it into practice – Our Thoughts

The thoughts I battled during postnatal depression were vicious and relentless. It felt like a constant repeating internal loop of crushing negativity and self-condemnation. I felt useless, worthless and defeated. God's view of me was totally different but it wasn't possible for me to connect with God's view of me through the thick, swirling fog in my thoughts.

In order to challenge my thoughts, I had to first slow them down and then press an internal "Pause" button after each one had run to give me time to question it. A condemning thought would run so fast and have so many little extra jibes associated with it I'd be reeling, and then another would immediately follow in its path. Something like this:

"You are such a failure as a parent. Other mums are doing so much more with their little ones and you can't even get the basics done at home and get yourself out of the house."

"The house is a mess. If you got yourself organised you'd be so much more efficient. You should have put the laundry on first so it could wash the clothes whilst you tidy up."

"You have never looked so awful. You still don't fit back in your pre-baby clothes. Are you going to do some exercise? When? You never feel like it. Are you going to get your hair done or keep tying it up in a ponytail every day? When was the last time you washed it?"

Faced with an internal onslaught like this I was quite literally unable to do anything. Slowing the accusations down in order to challenge them was a process in itself. I found focusing on one Bible verse helped and I shortened it so I could memorise it:

Philippians 4:13 (AMP):

> I have strength for all things in Christ Who empowers me [I am ready for anything and equal to anything through Him Who infuses inner strength into me . . .].

I shortened it to

> "I can do all things through Christ who strengthens me."

I'd repeat this over and over to block out the thoughts and make the internal storm die down. I didn't use it to convince myself I was healed. I used it to help me get dressed or change a nappy or put a load of washing on. Once my mind was calmer, I could cut myself some slack and see that I was just doing the best I could on very little sleep and no extra help. It didn't make me feel less frumpy or give me more energy but it did clear the head fog for a little while. If I drowned out my thoughts and forced myself to focus on what I was saying it certainly gave me some respite and perspective.

These two examples from David and Paul encourage us to actively combat *depressing emotions by speaking to them* and *depressing thoughts by wrangling them into submission in our head and replacing them with something true and positive*. It's important to recognise that doing this requires a certain level of energy and fight that some mums with severe symptoms may not have.

Attack No 3 – The Deep, Dark Pit

For those mums who suffer severe postnatal depression the attacks are emotional, mental and physical. Energy levels can be very low. It's like being locked in a prison. It is a deep, dark pit and you feel as though you sit alone on the ground at the bottom of it.

You feel unable to climb out by yourself, unworthy of being rescued and when you look upwards the sky above is full of dark clouds so why bother? The good news is that Jesus came as a light to the world's dark places, even the ones in our head; in fact, especially the dark places in our head.

Luke 1:78-79 (AMP) tells us:

> Because of and through the heart of tender mercy and loving-kindness of our God, a Light from on high will dawn upon us and visit [us].

> To shine upon and give light to those who sit in darkness and in the shadow of death, to direct and guide our feet in a straight line into the way of peace.

Oh my goodness how I needed someone to come with a light and find me in my dark place and guide me step by step in a straight line. Do you need the same? Do you long for some peace too? I certainly did and the Bible tells us it is on offer.

Sometimes the place we find ourselves is not one we can climb out of on our own. God knows that and He doesn't expect you to do this in your own strength, that's why He sent us His Son.

Putting it into practice – The Deep, Dark Pit

For me this depression and despair was so deep I just had to hand it all over to Jesus. I remember being alone in my house, but for my baby daughter, and sitting on my bedroom floor unable to get up. This verse wasn't theoretical for me, it was factual. The darkness might have been in my mind but it was still a prison. With my head in my hands all I could pray was:

"Jesus, I really need your help! Please come and get me out of this hole!"

My cry for help was short. I had nothing in the tank. I had no fight left. I was out of rope. In this situation Jesus knows He has to come to us and meet us where we are.

When He comes, don't feel you are expected to do anything. Just let Him sit down in the pit and join you and put His arm around you and love you. Let Him tell you how valuable you are. Let Him reassure you that you are doing a great job as a mum. Let Him tell you that you have all you need to be the parent your child needs. Let Him tell you He has plans for you and they are good plans. Let Him reassure you that you have a future that is so much better than where you are now.

When you are ready, when you've been comforted, when light has broken through the darkness, even if only a little, only then are you able to put your hand in His and get up off the ground and let Him lead you gently step by step through His Word towards recovery and healing.

Recovery and healing are not a one-size-fits-all. For you it might come through a variety of approaches. Reading your Bible helps deepen and strengthen your faith but when you don't know it too well it can feel alien to turn to it for help.

At this stage I was doing what many call "Bible Roulette". I was just praying for God to help me and opening it in some random place hoping it would be on something God wanted to share with me. Actually, more often than not, I found my eyes fell on something helpful. Give it a try.

Your Bible is the main way in which God can speak to you, so do try opening it and taking a look. If your Bible is written in old-style language that you don't connect with very easily then consider buying a more modern translation. It will help. A closed Bible can't do much, but an open Bible can change your life.

Your recovery might involve seeing your doctor. God often uses medicine as part of our healing process and He has blessed scientists with insight to make medical advances to help us. Perhaps counselling or a regular chat with someone who is supportive will enable you to turn a corner and keep going in a positive direction.

Music can reach deep inside us and uplift our spirits. The psalms in the Bible were written to be sung in the temple in Jerusalem. Many psalms even have footnotes describing the instruments the writer had in mind to accompany them. Today there are so many genres of Christian music you're sure to find a melody to suit your taste and lyrics to meet your need.

I've put a song suggestion at the end of this topic to get you started. "If We're Honest" by Francesca Battistelli really spoke to me about sharing my feelings, recognising we all have struggles and encouraged me not to hide my problems away.

In closing, David shows us how to speak to negative emotions and Paul instructs us to challenge and manage and replace depressive thoughts. Luke shows us that when we are at the end of our rope there is help, we can ask Jesus to sit and join us and we can lean on Him to help us to get up off the floor. We can put our hand into Jesus' hand and follow His light into peace.

Thankfully most women do make a full recovery from postnatal depression. It lifts gradually until you realise that you feel more positive about life, more balanced in your emotions day to day and recognise that you are a capable mother who is learning on the job just like everyone else.

In the meantime, as you journey towards restored mental health, I pray that the Holy Spirit, the ultimate counsellor, meets you and comforts you and guides you wherever you are.

Be blessed x

 Prayer

Heavenly Father,

Thank You for loving me regardless of how I feel about myself. Right now, the condemning thoughts and negative emotions of postnatal depression are trying to drag me under. I am struggling, Father, and I need Your help. I need a breakthrough and I know I can't get there on my own. Please, help me.

I am like a child in the dark. Just as Your Word says, please send Jesus to shine on me in my darkness and give me a light to hold. Give me a hope to cling to that will guide me through. Show me what help I need to break free from this.

Jesus, please sit with me, comfort me, and lead me back to a peaceful mind and a restored life.

Thank You,

Amen

 Recommended song

"If We're Honest" by Francesca Battistelli

Written by: Francesca Battistelli, Jeff Pardo, Molly E. Reed

This piano-based song has such a soothing melody. You can hear every word Francesca sings without difficulty and her lovely voice is in turn both soft and soaring. I knew straight away it was the right match for this topic. It's as though she saw my situation and wrote this song with lyrics that touched my heart. Struggling with postnatal depression, pretending I was ok whilst hiding how I was really feeling, was a very dark place to be indeed. This song shows us how opening up will release us from isolation. It reminds us that others suffer too and how Jesus longs to offer comfort. It was a balm to my soul. I hope it blesses you today.

Mum Memories

Your space to use as you choose.

Suggestion

Maybe you can write yourself an encouraging note to help you in the darker moments. Perhaps an uplifting poem, a strengthening Bible verse or a hope-filled prayer to remind you that your healing is coming.

Sleep Deprivation

Does your little one wake up during the night? Do they wake up often?

Lack of sleep is so common among mums it's considered part and parcel of parenting, especially in the first few months when babies can need feeding every 2 hours right around the clock.

But what is sleep deprivation? The sort of sleep deprivation that affects most mums is caused by:

- Lack of sleep i.e. fewer hours than you are used to getting.
- Interrupted sleep where you get up once or more in the night.
- Or a combination of the two where you get fewer hours and what little you do get is broken by one or more interruptions.

All three scenarios can play havoc with your health. Human sleep is a complex activity and most adults need between 7 and 9 hours of unbroken sleep each night in order to complete what are called "sleep cycles". These are phases of sleep that enable us to wake up feeling refreshed. We need between 4 and 6 sleep cycles per night and if these sleep cycles are interrupted and / or reduced we start to feel the effects of sleep deprivation.

There are many phases of child development that can result in sleep deprivation for parents. The most obvious and usually the most severe stage is that of a newborn whose tiny tummy needs regular filling in the first few months until they grow and the number of feeds reduces. But there are other phases of child development that can bring broken sleep for mum:

- Night terrors affect many small children. They have a nightmare and wake up distressed and in need of comfort in order to re-settle.

- Teething is of course famous for interrupting sleep.

- Viruses affect babies and children as they build their immune system. This is particularly unpleasant when a 3.00am wake up also involves changing vomit-stained bedding.

- As children grow you may find you have a particularly active child who doesn't seem to need much sleep at night and wakes at an antisocial hour in the morning full of life, noisily insisting that it's breakfast time (I have one of these).

- And, of course, we get added complications that affect our sleep such as being unable to get back to sleep ourselves after being woken up. We get up and tend to our little ones and then return to bed and lie awake unable to go back to sleep again for ages. This one is especially frustrating.

Sleep deprivation is one part of parenting that leaves lasting memories. If you are in this situation right now with an infant, older baby or even an older child who is still not sleeping through, then this *Mums Chat* topic is for you.

Sleep deprivation has very real effects on body, mind and spirit and I often found myself on autopilot – low on energy, devoid of patience, seemingly unable to do anything very taxing. My head was full of cotton wool and my limbs felt heavy without the weight of carrying my baby around. I dropped things regularly, I forgot words in the middle of talking, I'd forget what I'd walked upstairs to fetch, and my wit, charm and sparkling conversation disappeared.

I think the prophet Isaiah knew about sleep deprivation and the challenges of caring for a baby when he wrote in

Isaiah 40:1, 11 (AMP):

> Comfort, comfort My people, says your God.

> He will feed His flock like a shepherd: He will gather the lambs in His arm, He will carry them in His bosom and will gently lead those that have their young.

I was definitely a sleep-deprived mother sheep who was relieved and glad that the shepherd wanted to carry my beloved baby in His strong arms and lead me gently and slowly to follow Him.

I immediately think of another of my favourite sheepy verses.

Psalm 23:1-3 (AMP):

> The Lord is my Shepherd [to feed, guide, and shield me], I shall not lack.

> He makes me lie down in [fresh, tender] green pastures; He leads me beside the still and restful waters.

> He refreshes and restores my life . . .

The mere suggestion of a lie down in these verses is just lovely and I do hope that if you are a sleep-deprived mum that you give yourself permission to lie down when you have the chance. The housework can wait. Your battery needs a re-charge and this is far more important than the washing, ironing or cleaning. Fresh, tender, green pastures wait for you. As you close your eyes imagine the still and restful waters.

Night times were particularly challenging when my children were infants and long afterwards too. They woke at night, every night, and often more than once. In those early days, I decided to make it more bearable by setting myself a Chocolate Chip Cookie Challenge. I allowed myself to enjoy a cookie (just one) and some warm milk to help me get back to sleep when I'd settled my little one back down. Stood alone in my dimly lit kitchen, looking at the clock showing a number anywhere between 1 and 5 o'clock, it was always a tiny bit easier with my own little get-me-back-to-sleep routine.

I made it my personal mission to do some earnest quality testing in those wee small hours. Over time (and we are talking years not months) I munched my way through every major supermarket chocolate chip cookie brand in the UK. Of course, this method didn't always help me fall back to sleep instantly but those dark, lonely nights were definitely better for it and my tummy didn't grumble.

Day times were also a challenge because, unlike my tiny daughter (who could snooze for England), my super-charged son seemed to only need a half-hour power nap during the day. I lost count of the number of times I'd just dropped off to sleep alongside his cot only for him to wake up after 30 minutes fully refreshed. Amazingly, though, whenever I put myself in God's hands, whatever rest I'd had was enough – even if it was just lying down mid-afternoon for 10 minutes with my eyes closed. I found I had just enough energy to plod through moment to moment. Just.

I'm not claiming I could climb a mountain or even do the weekly grocery shop but I could get through to the end of the day.

 Putting it into practice

So how did I put myself in God's hands? I used these steps below and I hope they help you too.

Cast your burden

1) Psalm 55:22 (AMP) says:

> Cast your burden on the Lord [releasing the weight of it] and He will sustain you; He will never allow the [consistently] righteous to be moved (made to slip, fall, or fail).

So, as I lay down to get some sleep – regardless of when that was in the day or night – I would commit my rest to God reminding Him of His word saying:

> "Father, whatever rest I get now, please let it be enough."

And as I got up out of bed yet again, whenever it was, I said to Him:

> "Heavenly Father, I can't do this on my own, please help me."

"Casting my burden on the Lord" didn't mean I just lay on my bed saying a moany prayer. I had to honestly surrender to God my angst, my stress and deep, deep tiredness. I did often cry tears of utter exhaustion (and self-pity as I watched my husband sleeping undisturbed), but I knew God could be trusted to give me peace and stretch the benefits of my rest.

You can cast your burden on Him too. Breathe, relax and trust Him and just be still and know He will get you through moment to moment.

2) Be realistic about your To Do list

That may well involve altering your expectations of yourself and approaching things more slowly. It may require that you reduce your To Do list or scrap it all together for a while. Be realistic about what you can and can't do. This is a time to be kind to yourself. Say No when you need to say No to others. Say Yes to positive ways to support yourself – chocolate chip cookies worked for me.

3) Build rest into your schedule and expect it to get better over time

In closing, God promises that He will refresh and strengthen us in another wonderfully relevant verse for a sleep-deprived mum.

Isaiah 40:31 (AMP) reads:

> But those who wait for the Lord [who expect, look for and hope in Him] shall change and renew their strength and power; they shall lift their wings and

mount up [close to God] as eagles [mount up to the sun]; they shall run and not be weary, they shall walk and not faint or become tired.

Note what the eagles do. They do not flap their wings endlessly and exhaustingly. They don't rely on their own effort at all. They just raise their wings, much like a small child lifts their arms up to mummy or daddy to be picked up. They catch a thermal of warm air and they glide upwards without effort. This is how God's power can lift us when we rely on Him and not on our own effort.

Thankfully these intense periods of sleep deprivation don't last forever so if you are an exhausted mum, please know that you are not alone. Keep going. You're doing so well. This will end and you will get back to enjoying more sleep. In the meantime, "wait for the Lord; renew your strength and power through Him".

Go steady, be kind to yourself and be blessed x

 Prayer

Heavenly Father,

Thank You for the verse in Isaiah 40 – it shows me that You know how tiring it is having little ones. Thank You for the psalms that tell me You understand how much I need a rest.

I have not slept properly for a long time and I am struggling to keep going. As I lay my baby down for their night-time sleep or their day-time nap please let them settle quickly. As I lie down myself, please help me to see Jesus taking my little one in His arms so I can relax and know I am able to focus on my own needs for a while.

Father, help me to close my eyes, relax and breathe and picture the green grass by the restful stream. Please let the rest I get, even if it is brief, be enough to see me through the day.

In those moments when I need to get things done but my energy is low help me to remember to lean on You. Give me a realistic view of what I can do at this time and peace in my head and my heart if I need to let go of doing some things for a while.

I will trust You, Lord, to enable me to keep going because I know You are beside me. Show me how to lift my wings and just glide with Your help.

Amen

 Recommended song

"Find Rest" by Francesca Battistelli

Written by: Ian Eskelin, Jared Gordon Anderson, Francesca Battistelli

When I first heard this song I thought the opening lyrics were talking about a wakeful infant who would not drift off. But actually, this song starts by reminding us that God is always awake and watching over. For us mums it's reassuring to know He's doing this with love and care, recognising this is a difficult, tiring time.

This is a period when you are up frequently during the night, just you and your baby. Lonely hours. It reminds us that our heavenly Father knows we need rest for our body, mind and spirit and He can be relied upon, leaned upon to help and provide hope of better to come.

Mum Memories

Your space to use as you choose.

Suggestion

Time passes, seasons change and you will enjoy unbroken sleep again. During this challenging time how can you put yourself in His hands and be kind to yourself?

Body Image

Body image can be a huge source of stress for women generally, especially after giving birth. Having a baby brings so many personal changes: emotional, financial but the most obvious are physical. It doesn't matter who you are, having a baby changes your shape and your body ever after in one way or another.

At mother and baby groups you'll hear the topic of body image being discussed as new mums tell each other:

> *"I'm nowhere near getting back into my pre-baby clothes. I'm still wearing my maternity jeans!"*

And even though we know it takes 9 months to grow a baby we all hope to fit back into our pre-pregnancy clothes as quickly as possible after giving birth.

It doesn't help matters that we regularly see women in the public eye, such as royalty and celebrities, showing off their baby bump only to give birth, disappear from public view for a few months then reappear without any obvious signs of having been pregnant at all.

For most of us mums losing the baby weight takes a long time and it's more a process of discovering what shape and size we have become after childbirth than recovering our pre-pregnancy silhouette.

I have a small frame but I went up a size after giving birth to my daughter and didn't go back down again. I went up another size in having my son and now I'm sort of in between sizes with some things too tight and some things too baggy. It takes time to find your new normal and it can take even longer to reach self-acceptance. Some of us will spring back into a shape we are happy with over a few months and others of us will really struggle with the permanent after-effects of pregnancy.

It's not just our body shape that changes during pregnancy and childbirth. There are lots of other very common side effects that we all know about but they don't feature on social media or in glossy magazines.

Shortly after my daughter was born my ankles and lower legs became terribly swollen and I hobbled around because my shoes were so tight. It only lasted a week or so but it left me with a significant number of thread veins on my legs. It's taken me a long time to come to terms with them, especially in the summer when they are on display. But I decided to call them my Ania tattoos after my daughter and now I'm kind of fond of them.

In a similar way, since having my children there are certain situations that are now rather problematic. For example, a full bladder and an unexpected sneeze are not a good combination for me. A friend of mine with four young children admitted recently that she has given herself a "three-bounce limit" on her children's garden trampoline for similar reasons. And another mum confided that her once magnificent bosom had shrunk significantly since having her three boys.

Taking all this into consideration:

- change of body shape during pregnancy,

- milk production after birth,

- ongoing physical recovery after childbirth

- and pressure to get back in shape and look fabulous all the time

it's no wonder body image becomes an issue for so many mums after childbirth. Most of us try to ignore it but wearing maternity clothes day in and day out after your baby has arrived isn't much fun. We are so busy caring for our little ones that wearing clothes that are relatively comfortable and relatively clean is as far as we get. Accessories, make-up and perfume bottles often gather dust in our bedroom. And how we feel about our body shape is not an area we venture into too often because it's not a good place – it's a dark place – with no mirrors!

Well Genesis has a little to say about how God views us and remember He created us naked.

Genesis 1:26-28 (AMP):

God said, Let Us [Father, Son, and Holy Spirit] make mankind in Our image, after Our likeness, and let them have complete authority over the fish of the sea, the birds of the air, the [tame] beasts, and over all the earth . . .

So God created man in His own image . . . male and female He created them.

And God blessed them and said to them, Be fruitful, multiply, and fill the earth . . .

Note, God didn't say be fruitful and multiply and fit back in your jeans in 8 weeks. Verse 31 concludes beautifully with:

And God saw everything that He had made, and behold, it was very good (suitable and pleasant) and He approved it completely.

It makes me smile that God looks at my naked shape now I've had my babies (and let's face it, I can't hide from Him in the bathroom), and He finds it suitable and pleasant and He approves of it completely. In the eyes of my Creator my post-pregnancy body shape is very good. And so is yours.

The Bible tells me that God loves me completely just as I am. And He loves you too. If I spend the next few months doing a daily workout with a fitness DVD in my lounge, He'll love me just the same and approve of my shape just as much. And you've guessed it – the same applies to you too.

I do still hide a wobbly post-pregnancy tummy in my jeans and at some point I may decide to exercise in order to lose it, not to mention toning up my pelvic floor. In the meantime, I'm going to keep reminding myself to be thankful that my body has been blessed to do an incredible job in creating two lovely babies and, whilst it looks very different since, it still works well enough.

I hope you are patient with yourself as you discover your new "normal" and I hope the section below helps with the tricky area of body image and self-acceptance, because while outward appearance is important to most of us, it isn't to God.

Putting it into practice

This is probably the longest "putting it into practice" section in this book because this is such a big issue and if you are anything like me you'll need to revisit it over and over. I've had a lot of practice at "putting it into practice" and I know I'll get a lot more as I get older. So, what factors can we consider as we try to find a new way of thinking on this subject? Firstly, let's dig a little into why body image is such a challenge for us and then we will apply some truth, kindness and Bible-based support to help bring a breakthrough.

1) Our comparison culture

I'm convinced that this body image struggle is part of being human so please don't think you are the only one who looks in the mirror and sometimes frowns at their reflection. And please don't think this is a "one and done" process that you will find the answer and then get on with life. It doesn't work like that.

Our culture tells us from the earliest age that how we look is a defining part of our value. We often find that we compare ourselves to others and decide privately if we measure up.

The scripting starts for girls almost immediately. The beautiful fairy-tale princess always gets her prince. The picture-perfect (usually photo-filtered) social media influencer has her adoring followers and is showered with free gifts to try out on her personal channel.

Luxury brands often still create adverts using mainly tall, thin models whose bodies don't reflect mainstream society. And whilst we know logically that it is all the shallow veneer of marketing trying to sell us something, be it a product or an image or a lifestyle, it hooks a deep need within us to belong and be liked.

It's no wonder that our own self-acceptance is often significantly rooted in what we think about our body and how we compare ourselves to others.

Our culture is not going to change so we will need to learn to fight against the temptation to compare ourselves to others and learn strategies to help us do that.

2) The judgement of others

Having a baby is a major event and brings with it, both during pregnancy and afterwards, all sorts of flash points relating to:

- how you see yourself and possibly
- how you think your husband or partner sees you now too

and for a single mum

- how you might assume a potential future husband / partner will see you.

Some of us have found that people, who we hoped would be supportive, have actually been dismissive or unkind as we grapple with the demands of a new baby and all that comes with our new arrival plus a changed body shape. Please keep reading. You will find truth, kindness and Bible-based support here.

Truth

Whilst we keep our focus on ourselves and what other people think we won't find a way through this. What is so often missing is taking a step back from the mirror, the selfies, the constant comparisons and assumptions and seeing yourself as God sees you.

And it's worth repeating that putting this into practice requires exactly that – lots of practice – because this is one challenge we are likely to have to come back to time and again.

Kindness

Here I'm referring to self-kindness. Have you taken time out to really look at how far you've come already? Can I share something private? When I was nearly 9 months pregnant with my son I locked myself in my bathroom and took a photo of myself in the mirror wearing just my underwear. It wasn't a photo that I wanted to share with others. It was just to remind me in the months ahead just how enormous my stomach had been. Truly huge! I'm glad that I took it because I've used it on several occasions since to look back (on those grey self-critical days) to see how far I've come. Please don't misunderstand me; I still have a wobbly tummy and I won't be wearing a bikini on the beach anytime soon, but that photo has helped me many times to regain my perspective whenever I've felt overly self-critical and consumed by negativity. My body has been through a lot. My new normal is different but I am healthy. That's enough.

Here's the Bible-based support that brings a body image breakthrough. Are you ready? Let's go . . .

1) It really is what's on the inside that counts

Body image still matters to me but far less than it used to. I've cut myself some slack. I'm not perfect. I never will be and nobody else is perfect either. And from a faith perspective what is on the outside is shown time and again to be unimportant.

God sees straight past your hairstyle and hang-ups. He homes in on your heart.

1 Samuel 16:7 (AMP):

> The Lord sees not as man sees; for man looks on the outward appearance, but the Lord looks on the heart.

He values the inner person. It is a beautiful thing to Him. You are beautiful to God. Maybe you need to read this over and over till it starts to really register. Just as you are, you are beautiful in the eyes of your Maker.

2) You were created unique and for an individual God-given purpose

When you were formed inside your mother's womb God saw you in the darkness and He loved you. He still does. He has gifted you and equipped you in a unique way to accomplish a plan that was designed for you alone. No one else can step in and do it instead of you. This plan is not linked to your body image; it is linked to who you are on the inside, who you were created to be. So, comparison to others is a waste of time. We each have a unique plan designed for us alone.

Jeremiah 1:5 (AMP) puts this so very well:

Before I formed you in the womb I knew [and] approved of you [as My chosen instrument], and before you were born I separated and set you apart, consecrating you; [and] I appointed you as a prophet to the nations.

Now this verse applies to each of us, not just Jeremiah. I was not born to be an Old Testament prophet, but equally Jeremiah wasn't born to write *Mums Chat* and neither he nor I can bring to the world what only you can bring. We each have our own God-given plan. Just imagine if we redirected our time and energy into fearlessly chasing down our unique, heaven-designed, life plan instead of worrying about our body image – how much better would our lives be?

3) Think about it – no one knows what Jesus looked like

The Bible makes no mention of Jesus' appearance anywhere because it wasn't what defined Him. As a result, we have various images of your typical Jesus figure from around the world as sculptors and artists try to imagine what He looked like and try to bring Him to life for us.

Sometimes He is depicted as being blond haired with blue eyes and pale skin. I've seen other Jesus figures with brown hair, brown eyes and darker skin.

But what really brings Jesus to life is not knowing what He might have looked like when He was here on earth but having a personal friendship with Him now through your prayers and seeing them answered.

4) Get your self-worth rooted in a higher place

What really brings you to life is freedom from self-judgement and the judgement of others. When you accept that you are a precious child of God you become plugged into the security of always being loved, always belonging, always being accepted and having a purpose beyond your external image.

We won't change the fact that people will still judge us based on how we look because that is part of how our society operates. But the importance we attach to that and how it impacts on our own self-acceptance is for us to decide and work on. Our challenge is keeping ourselves plugged into that higher place.

If we turn away from the mirror and look to God we will see He offers us His all-embracing love. A love that is unshakeable. A love that we can rely upon.

It can take a while for this realisation to sink in (a lifetime maybe) but as it does trickle down into our hearts, we can gradually make body image less and less important over time as we practise again and again seeing ourselves as God sees us and valuing ourselves as God values us.

External beauty will fade over time but internal beauty will always shine.

Prayer

Heavenly Father,

Thank You for my baby. Thank You for my body that was able to carry my child. Thank You that childbirth is over and I can focus on being a mum.

Father God, I know I have so much to be grateful for and yet, instead of counting my blessings, I often find myself looking in the mirror and counting what I think are my defects. It makes me feel so low.

I know recovery from pregnancy and childbirth takes a long time. I accept that my body will be altered in some ways permanently, but I am finding it very hard right now to be positive about how I look. Certain aspects make me feel very down on myself.

Help me, Father, to take my gaze away from scrutinising how I look and instead focus on You. You tell me that outward appearances are not what catches Your eye at all. It's my heart that You are looking at.

You are not judging me by the world's standards and deciding whether I fit and whether I am acceptable. You already decided that You love me. You already decided that I belong. You already call me Your daughter. And You will always feel this way about me. You have a plan for my life that is unique to me and totally unrelated to how I look.

Help me to connect with that assurance and security when I feel vulnerable. When I fall back into the habit of racking up my body image failings, please remind me to refocus. Help me to practise seeing myself as You do and find rest in Your acceptance.

I ask this in Jesus' name,

Amen

 Recommended song

"True Beauty" by Mandisa

Written by: Mandisa Hundley, Lavonne Cindy Morgan, Andrew Maxwell Ramsey

Mandisa became famous after taking part in *American Idol* back in 2005 where she was publicly subjected, on stage, to hurtful comments about her body shape by Simon Cowell. Despite the pain he caused, Mandisa rose above, publicly forgiving Simon. Mandisa went on to become a Grammy Award winner with a super successful music career. In 2007 she released an album entitled *True Beauty* and this track superbly addresses the body image challenge we all face. It might have been released a few years ago but the lyrics pack a punch.

You might be familiar with this song or it might be the first time you have ever heard it, but it captures what really matters and repeats the truth that our Creator God looks at our heart not our appearance. In Him we find the freedom to be ourselves and know we are loved just as we are. I hope you enjoy it as much as I do.

Mum Memories

Your space to use as you choose.

Suggestion

When body image worries start to niggle at you, how can you press "Pause" in that moment and stop? How has God gifted you, on the inside, to make this world a better place?

Bouncing Baby Section

Welcome to the Bouncing Baby section. Just as you think you are getting to grips with being a parent your tiny baby grows and enters a new phase of development. Sitting up, smiling, exploring and teething become the new topics of conversation at mum and baby groups. The Bouncing Baby section addresses some of the common niggling doubts that can creep into your mind during this phase, both about yourself and your baby. Together we will unlock biblical truth to combat the barbed comments of others and arm you to deal effectively with negative self-talk. Our battles are best fought with scripture and for each of these different struggles you will find Bible verses to help you come out fighting.

Again, please make the time to download the recommended songs after each section. Praise is powerful and worship is warfare and these songs have been purposefully chosen to help you speak God's truth over your situation till you see your victory.

Here are the topics covered and the recommended songs:

Baby Milestones and Competitive Mothers

Recommended song

"Stars In The Sky" by Kari Jobe

Lost Identity

Recommended song

"In Your Eyes" by Hillsong Young and Free

Teething

Recommended song

"In My Arms" by Plumb

Guilty Mother Syndrome

Recommended song

"Freedom" by Jesus Culture (New Song Café version)

If you would like a personal video-based "Hello and welcome!" to this section, please scan the QR code or follow the link below and, via my website, you'll be transported to the *Mums Chat* kitchen.

https://mumschat.thinkific.com/courses/bouncing-baby

Baby Milestones and Competitive Mothers

It's true of all parents that, once our new baby has arrived, we watch with curiosity for indications that developmental milestones are being reached. For first-time parents especially, these milestones are signals that their baby is developing normally. They give peace of mind (as well as bringing fresh challenges). From cute infant reflexes such as finger grabbing and sucking to the first smile at around 12 weeks we are constantly observing and noticing progress.

At 6 months we are looking for signs that weaning can start and, as time moves on, teething and crawling and walking and talking follow – though not necessarily in that order. There's a lot to look out for and there are countless baby books and parenting websites all telling us what our child should be doing as they grow and when.

And as you watch for signs in your own baby you can't help noticing how your friends' babies are developing too. The temptation to compare your baby favourably, for being ahead, or unfavourably if another child is ahead, is very real and it's habit forming. Underneath it all is relief on the one hand that baby is moving on and worry on the other hand that they are late because something is wrong.

It's around this time that Competitive Mother Syndrome can start to raise its ugly head. I'm sure you've met the type at mother and baby groups. Celebrating your baby's milestones is natural and sharing the news is normal but there is always an edge to the way competitive mothers share their news that seems to indicate a smug superiority and leaves other mothers watching their own child and privately questioning and worrying if their child is ok.

The reality is that every child will develop at his or her own pace. Accepting that can be tricky, especially for new mums who are bombarded with books, blogs, websites and possibly family and friends all advising what "normal" is. In fact, normal infant development is measured along a bandwidth and not with specific dates. There are huge variances in when children develop and reach their milestones, and all are regarded as normal, for example:

- babies can start to teeth as early as 3 months and equally they can still be gummy on their first birthday.

- babies can start to sleep through the night after only a few months, to the jubilation of their parents, only to start waking up again.

- babies can be born with a full head of hair and it can all subsequently fall out and grow back, when its ready, and be a completely different colour.

- equally a baby can be completely bald and not grow a full head of hair until well past his or her first birthday.

None of this would worry a health professional.

So, if you want to stand on God's Word when someone tries to steal your peace about your baby's milestones where can you go?

Well Psalm 73 (AMP) can teach us a lot. If you read the first part, King David was basically having a rant. He was very annoyed about proud, prosperous, Godless people who, in his words:

Verse 8:

> They scoff, and wickedly utter oppression; they speak loftily [from on high, and maliciously and blasphemously].

This could very well be King David's version of having his buttons pushed by a competitive mother. Basically, he was very cross with how these people had spoken.

In verse 21 he says:

> For my heart was grieved, embittered, and in a state of ferment, and I was pricked in my heart [as with the sharp fang of an adder].

It really sounds as though he had let these people work him into quite a lather.

In verse 22 he describes what he must have looked like as he was spitting feathers in the sanctuary of God.

> So foolish, stupid, and brutish was I, and ignorant; I was like a beast before You.

And then he calms down and in verses 23 to 26 he gives us what we need to hear.

> Nevertheless, I am continually with You. You do hold my right hand.

> You will guide me with Your counsel, and afterward receive me to honour and glory.

Whom have I in heaven but You? And I have no delight or desire on earth besides You.

My flesh and my heart may fail, but God is the Rock and firm Strength of my heart and my Portion forever.

So when someone tries to steal your peace and push your buttons about baby milestones remember you can hold God's hand. He will guide you with His counsel and His wisdom, and though we may fail and get rattled or worried, because we are human, God is still our Rock and the firm Strength or our heart. So, stand on the Rock and do not be shaken. Keep your peace as your baby grows. God has designed his or her development plan. Rest in that knowledge and be blessed x

 Putting it into practice

"Keep your peace as your baby grows" is a great bit of advice and "resting in the knowledge that God has your child's development plan all mapped out" is a great place to be but how do you do that exactly?

My buttons were definitely pushed over my baby daughter's development and I can remember coming home in a rage after a visit to a local mum and baby group. My daughter, Ania, never really learned to crawl, she just rolled everywhere and usually got quite dusty and dirty in the process. That day another mum at the baby group I went to had stood next to me and watched my daughter traversing the carpet in her own unique style. Ania "did her thing" and rolled over and over to get to where she wanted to go. The mother next to me then commented how her child had mastered crawling and as a result was developing limb muscles in readiness for walking. Then she walked off to get a cup of tea.

I'm not sure if the comment was supposed to make me feel worried or embarrassed. Often these comments are so subtle they've been said and the other mum has gone before the verbal smack in the face registers. But I sure came away feeling that, in her eyes, I was the mother of a less than perfect baby and her child was superior to mine. I was so cross! Partly I was angry that another mum could be snidely critical of my baby and partly I was angry with myself for taking the bait. Oh, but take the bait I did – it went right down into my heart. There's a Bible verse describing exactly that feeling of when ill-chosen words of others really irk us. It was written by King Solomon in

Proverbs 18:18 (DRA):

> The words of the double-tongued are as if they were harmless: and they reach even to the inner parts of the bowels.

I'm sure you've had a similar experience yourself and it really stays with you, doesn't it?

Well, a quick internet lookup at home showed me that rolling was quite normal and in due course, over the 12 months that followed, Ania went straight to pulling herself up, cruising and then walking. She wasn't behind in her milestones or abnormal at all. But that particular day was tricky for me.

So, what were the steps I needed to follow to put this "trusting God for my baby's development" into practice? I've noted them here and I definitely recommend them to you.

1) Be quick to forgive, for your own sake

Firstly, I needed to forgive the person who had angered me. Thankfully forgiveness is a decision long before it becomes a feeling. I knew I needed to let go of this for my own benefit because it was frothing me up on the inside and basically ruining my day and I wanted to get my nice day back.

This woman was probably at home by now and had forgotten me completely. I might never see her again so waiting for an apology was a waste of my time. A great many of my forgiveness prayers have been through gritted teeth and this was no exception.

Heavenly Father,

I forgive that mum for being unkind. Please help me to put it behind me and move on from what she said to me. I trust You to oversee Ania's development.

Amen

2) Do some research

Secondly, I needed to do my research to see if I actually had any cause for concern – which I discovered I didn't. That helped me so much. If you need reassurance on anything to do with baby milestones, then contacting your doctor or health visitor or other medical professional will give you the information you need.

3) Relax + Refocus = Resilience

Thirdly, I needed to get myself a long-term view. Baby milestones are important and we will notice them as they happen but spending every day anxiously watching out for them encourages us to micro manage our baby. There's no fun in that. I needed to relax, which for a first-time mum was not so easy, just enjoy my day and breathe and refocus on something else. Calling my mum helped. The saying "A trouble shared is a trouble halved" certainly rang true for me.

I hope this has given you some ideas to help you become spiritually resilient because competitive mothers exist at every stage of mothering and we need to get the skills to deal with them early on.

A lovely mum I know has two grown daughters who are both currently studying at university. One of her oldest friends recently said to her:

"I'm surprised that both your girls have gone to uni. I really didn't think they would."

Ouch! These jibes can come at any time of life and having a toolkit to move past them is so valuable.

Let's add a powerful prayer and a song about the night sky to your toolkit.

 Prayer

Heavenly Father,

I am so glad that You are alongside me in my parenting. I am thankful that I can see these competitive mother comments for what they are – an unkind attempt to steal my peace of mind. I know that the people who say these spiteful things actually need help because they must have been hurt by someone else to strike out as they do. I pray that You send them the help they need.

Father God, please help me to forgive and to remember that You have a good future in store for my child. You plotted their days before they were even born.

Jeremiah 29:11 tells me that You have a plan for each of us and those plans are to prosper us, not to harm us and to give us a hope and a future.

Whether my baby hits their baby milestones or not You still have a plan for them and You promise that it is a good plan. Please give me the resilience I need to overcome this challenge. Please give me the ability to put my child's future into Your hands and know You are the overseer of it all.

You see the beginning and the end and You love my child more than I do. Please restore my peace of mind as I go about my day.

I will trust You because You can be trusted.

Amen

 Recommended song

"Stars In The Sky" by Kari Jobe

Written by: Chris August, Kari Brooke Jobe

Kari Jobe is another world-famous, multi-award-winning Christian singer and songwriter. Kari's voice is truly soulful, and her songs are reflections of her devoted heart searching for God during her trials and praising Him in her victories. For me this song speaks so well into the trial of baby milestones and competitive mothers and helps us to lift our gaze up to Him.

Our heavenly Father cares for all of His creation and this song gives us a sense of perspective. If He is mighty enough to hold the stars in the sky then we can trust Him with our future and our children's future and give it over to Him. He's "got this" both for me and for you and our little ones too.

Mum Memories

Suggestion

Your space to use as you choose.

When did you last look at the stars in the sky? Where do you get the best view of them where you live? Your heavenly Father is holding the stars and He will hold you too, if you let Him.

Lost Identity

I often hear new mums admit:

"I love my baby but since she was born I've stopped being me and now I'm just someone's mum."

"What about me?"

"I sometimes feel like my work as a mum is mundane, monotonous and menial."

I'm sure your family has been enriched beyond measure by the arrival of your child. I bet your life has also been turned upside down and your home resembles a badly organised garage sale. You know what I'm describing. Your house seemingly shrinks as it accommodates everything you need to look after and entertain your new arrival.

Loss of identity is felt even more keenly today as many women have enjoyed a career prior to having children and feel their identity is linked to their work. The contrast between the ordered world of work and your world once a baby enters it is dramatic and sudden.

I'm sure you do thank God for your beautiful child but when you are alone at home endlessly doing the washing, putting dishes away, changing nappies and rinsing poo stains out of yet another white Babygro negative thoughts can creep into your head. Thoughts like:

- When am I going to get back to doing something more meaningful?

- I've lost my sense of self.

- I am an intelligent woman but I'm not using my intelligence. Is it even still there?

I had all these thoughts myself and at the bottom of it was, "What about me?"

It sounds selfish but when you are the one dealing with the feeding, the nappies and the seemingly endless sleepless nights it's a question that quite rightly comes up. In the middle of one of my "What about me?" moments I read Matthew 18:2 and 5 (AMP). Matthew wrote:

And He [Jesus] called a little child to Himself and put him in the midst of them,

Whoever receives and accepts and welcomes one little child like this for My sake and in My name receives and accepts and welcomes Me.

When I think of my work as a mum in light of this verse it causes me to re-assess the value of it. In a world that admires the stylish celebrity mum and celebrates the super successful business mum there is great comfort in being a spiritually assured mum, biblically anchored to the truth and God's promises.

Jesus said: "Blessed are the humble for theirs is the kingdom of heaven" (Matthew 5:3). Surely in today's "have it all – do it all" world being a mum at home raising little one(s) is humble. So surely, the kingdom of heaven belongs, in part, to mums.

James 4:10 (AMP) says:

Humble yourselves [feeling very insignificant] in the presence of the Lord, and He will exalt you [He will lift you up and make your lives significant].

So back to the challenge of lost identity. Jesus tells us that all the selfless work we do for our little ones, we do for Him. And that the humble own the kingdom of heaven. James tells us that if we humble ourselves we can trust the Lord to lift us up and make our lives significant. Babies and pre-schoolers grow. Their early years are a challenging season, but the season passes. We know it's a blessing and a privilege to be a mum and it's a tough assignment too. If this lost identity struggle strikes a chord with you then just know you are doing the greatest, most influential work of your life right now, at home.

Be blessed. Trust God. He will lift you up. You are significant.

 Putting it into practice

This is another long "putting it into practice" section because lost identity is such a universal issue among women who have become a mother, and for a first-time mum the loss of identity challenge can be quite acute. It was for me.

Up until motherhood we often find our identity is linked to our qualifications, our life experience, our hobbies and our work. Our circle of friends, our family and colleagues know us from the spheres of life we have in common with them. Conversations during a typical week vary depending upon which circle you are in and this provides positive stimulation for your emotional wellbeing. It reinforces that there are many facets to your personality and abilities. You are a rounded individual able to participate successfully in a variety of settings.

For me becoming a mother meant I was suddenly very much more housebound and on my own with my baby. The change was instant. Suddenly I was only going to places where the common ground between me and the others I met was, initially at least, being a parent. I didn't yet feel confident as a parent and those areas of my life where I did feel confident, I wasn't part of anymore.

Three things really help to overcome this Lost Identity feeling:

1) Getting a helicopter view

It's really important to get a helicopter view of this lost identity challenge because in fact you really haven't lost anything. In my work as a maternity coach I reassure mums that everything they feel they used to be is still inside them, it's just taking a rest while they learn to be a mum.

- If they decide to return to the world of work outside the home, they will rediscover their professional expertise and remember what they used to do.
- As their baby grows, they will be able to recommence their hobbies, activities and interests and possibly start new ones too.

It's the intensity and all-encompassing nature of early motherhood that seems, for a while, to stifle the other aspects of life that previously brought you variety. So yes, motherhood does sometimes seem monotonous and mundane and menial. And if we associate our "who" with our "do" then that linkage tells us we have lost our identity. We now feel we are a single dimensional person called Mum. When you look at it this way it's understandable to sometimes say, "What about me?" Please don't feel guilty if you do. I felt that way myself.

Getting that higher up, helicopter view of your life and knowing that, in time, you will get back to doing the other things you used to enjoy helps. There will be a time in the future when being a mum is just a *part* of who you are and what you do and not *all* of who you are and what you do.

2) Look in the rear-view mirror

Imagine yourself 10 years from now and take a moment to look back over this season of your life. Whilst we are in the thick of early-years parenting it's difficult sometimes to appreciate the blessing that this 24/7 experience is bringing to you and the blessing you are being to your child. But pick up any child psychology book and the 1-to-1 time you are investing in your baby today plays a huge part in their development both now and later. Your bonding, nurturing, educating, loving, nursing and boundary setting are all needed from the very start. Every day, in all you are doing, and especially in the repetition of routine, you are placing down the relational building blocks your child needs. This is really very valuable. Don't underestimate it. Keep going!

3) Don't confuse your spiritual "who" with your earthly "do"

Jesus made a point of giving parenting the high praise it deserves and making it clear to His disciples how important it is. I repeat what I wrote earlier: it is a privilege, a blessing and also a tough assignment. But the Bible goes further and encourages us to disassociate our intrinsic value from what we do and actually see ourselves set apart from it. Our "do" does not translate into the value of our "who" in the spiritual.

Our value is linked to being God's child and if that is our start point then nothing about our "do" can shake or diminish the value of our "who".

1 John 3:1 (NIV):

> See what great love the Father has lavished on us, that we should be called children of God! And that is what we are!

I'm a daughter of the Almighty, entitled to all the promises in the Bible during my time on earth, in the here and now, and assured of everlasting life in heaven once my time here is done. That is my foundational identity.

Of course, I still mix up my heavenly "who" and my earthly "do" on a regular basis. It's something I have to come back to time and again, like the body image challenge earlier. But deep down I know I belong to God; I am His child. That is my identity and it gives me great comfort to remind and re-remind myself of that when I forget.

A butterfly doesn't miss its previous identity as a caterpillar. Motherhood is morphing you into more than you were before, not less. And you will always be His.

Prayer

Heavenly Father,

Thank You for blessing me with a child. Thank You for giving me this opportunity to become a mother. I am so grateful.

Father, forgive me when I get frustrated with the narrowness and repetition of this season. Help me to shift my gaze from seeing this time as all there is and remember it fits into the wider context of my life. Help me to appreciate the great benefit that this concentrated time investment and focus is bringing to my baby and to me.

Finally, Father, please help me to see my identity as, first and foremost, my relationship to You. You call me "daughter". You lift my head and draw me close. You see my life from the beginning to the end and You know the significance of each day.

Help me to see that too and learn to separate my spiritual "who" from my earthly "do". I have not lost my identity. It was always based in who I am to You.

Thank You, Father,

Amen

Recommended song

"In Your Eyes" by Hillsong Young and Free

Written by: Benjamin Hastings, Ben Tan

Hillsong Young and Free present a live version of this song performed in Sydney, and it's a combination of the lyrics, the stage effects behind the singers and the main performer's passion that make this song my recommendation for this topic. Our sense of identity is so very much influenced by what we see around us, how we compare ourselves to others and measure ourselves based on what the world shouts is important.

This song is a keyboard anthem to lifting your gaze higher and focusing on Jesus as He gazes back at you. It's a rallying call to reject the worldly things that try to dazzle and derail us and instead treasure our true identity, through Jesus, as children of God.

Mum Memories

Your space to use as you choose.

Suggestion

Maybe you can make something like a pro's and con's list. Give it a title of "My Identity" and label one column "My Earthly Do" and the other column "My Heavenly Who". What would you put in each column?

Teething

I'm imagining the pained expression on your face because teething is a challenging time for all involved – for baby, for mum and for anyone who comes within earshot. I once heard a quip about how lucky Adam and Eve were to be created as adults and not to have to suffer teething. So true!

This is another rite of passage that our babies endure and we, as parents, endure alongside them. I understand it is possible for some children to pass through the process of teething without even noticing it – but I've never met one.

Most babies experience a variety of teething symptoms to some degree or other including red, hot cheeks, uncontrollable dribble or drooling, biting down on pretty much anything to gain relief, irritability, sleep disruption, mouth pain, loss of appetite. Teething often also brings with it severe nappy rash because poo and wee become more acidic.

And teething can also trigger conjunctivitis eye infections and earache. It's no wonder the poor little things cry. It's no wonder we mothers feel challenged as we nurse our babies through. And can someone please tell me why is it that teething seems to be more painful at night?

We try all sorts of remedies, teething gels, fridge-cooled dummies, cold raw carrot sticks, paracetamol or ibuprofen. Then there are the cute neckerchiefs and bibs to catch the endless drool, plus the cream for their chin as the drool makes their face sore.

And we quickly learn to change nappies as soon as they are soiled to avoid little bottoms getting burned and we apply generous amounts of cream to protect them. For most mums teething is a challenging, sleep-deprived time and you wonder when this upset, demanding, grumpy, tired baby will go and the sweet-natured baby you know will return.

Obviously, your sweet-natured baby will return at some point, but it can take months.

Teething seems to progress in phases. Adorable little front teeth usually arrive first, then we have a much-needed pause before the other teeth erupt each in their turn. I remember saying I was going to throw a party once my son was the other side of the process. Which reminds me . . . I still need to do that!

From start to finish it is an endurance test so what positives can we lean on as we go and what can the Bible offer us in terms of support at this tricky time? Well, here are five big positives:

1) Firstly, it's a normal developmental milestone and therefore to be celebrated. Your baby is growing and needs more than a pure milk diet, so teeth are vital.

2) Secondly, the teething process helps us as mothers to master the art of comforting our baby. It teaches us compassion as we put ourselves in their shoes and try to relieve the discomfort they can't communicate in words. Offering comfort is a truly biblical behaviour and teething gives us the chance to please God enormously.

2 Corinthians 1:3-4 (AMP) speaks of God's comfort to us and how we are supposed to pay it forward to others.

Blessed be the God and Father of our Lord Jesus Christ, the Father of sympathy (pity and mercy) and the God [Who is the Source] of every comfort (consolation and encouragement),

Who comforts (consoles and encourages) us in every trouble (calamity and affliction), so that we may also be able to comfort (console and encourage) those who are in any kind of trouble or distress.

Some verses in the Bible are tricky to understand but this isn't one of them – God's desire for us to comfort others is very clear and we make Him smile when we do it.

3) The third positive is a by-product of showing compassion. As we really try to understand what sort of pain our baby is feeling we become educated. Teething familiarises us with how our children behave when they are in pain. Their cry changes pitch, their temperament alters. We start to learn from their behaviours whether they have pain in their mouth, as indicated by biting down to relieve pressure, or whether in fact they are telling us they have an earache by pulling down on their ear lobes. This is knowledge worth having when they can't tell us what hurts.

4) This leads to the fourth positive, which is also a by-product of showing compassion and kind of like a free gift from your baby to you.

In showing compassion and offering comfort to your child when they are suffering it strengthens the bond of trust that your baby feels towards you. Turn it around and remember a time when you were in trouble or pain and you prayed to God and He brought you comfort. Remember how His care for you deepened your trust in Him. Caring for your baby during teething creates the same feelings of trust from them towards you. This is precious relationship building.

5) Then finally there is a fifth positive in this situation. Teething teaches us endurance. If you are nursing your baby through the teething process now then Colossians 1:11 (AMP) is for you.

[We pray] that you may be invigorated and strengthened with all power according to the might of His glory, [to exercise] every kind of endurance and patience.

Teething is a tricky time but we learn so much as we go through it. It is possible that, at some point, your child will become sick with a 24-hour virus. Their body will fight it off and their immune system will be strengthened as a result. When this happens, we as mothers are much better prepared to support our child due to the teething process and what it teaches us.

Teething hardens us to difficulties and teaches us to endure.

Isaiah 41:10 (AMP) says exactly that:

I am your God. I will strengthen and harden you to difficulties, yes, I will help you; yes, I will hold you up and retain you with My [victorious] right hand of rightness and justice.

So, if you are enduring the teething process with your baby be encouraged and have hope.

It's a natural progression milestone.

It teaches you compassion.

It educates you on the signs that young children send out when they can't tell you what's wrong.

It deepens your relationship with your child

Although it may be extremely testing at the time it doesn't last forever and it is a truly valuable learning, stretching, hardening experience for mums.

Be assured – your heavenly Father will help you. He will hold you up and retain you with His victorious right hand.

In the meantime, keeping going, grab at the positives and enjoy your baby's super cute toothy grin.

 Putting it into practice

We've looked at some of the positives of teething to help put a silver lining on this temporary cloud but how do you cope when your baby's teething has you at your wits' end? There comes a point for many mums when you've reached the end of your rope with the crying, the grumpiness, the clinginess, the lack of sleep, the inability to get anything done and the constant daily merry-go-round of pain-relief solutions offered and rejected. This section is not about your baby at all. This "putting it into practice" section is all about taking care of you, so you are able to take care of your baby.

1) Know that you are not alone

It seems I pushed my own mum to her limits when, many years ago, I was teething. She recalled that we'd stayed overnight at a friend's house on our journey up-country to visit family. Mum was mortified that I cried all night and kept everyone awake but there was nothing she could do. The experience clearly made a lasting impression on her. You are not alone in feeling this is a tough time. Every generation of new parents finds it testing.

2) Take a break

If you find you really need a break then ask someone for help. Even if it just gives you half an hour to go for a walk and clear your head or maybe grab 10 minutes to have a hot cup of tea out of earshot somewhere quiet.

Alternatively, ask someone you trust to take your baby out in the pram for a walk whilst you stay home and rest. It will do your baby good to get some fresh air, even if they cry the whole time they are out. You can't expect yourself to run on empty, so do take a break.

3) Enlist someone to support and comfort you

There is a well-known, old African saying that "it takes a village to raise a child". This saying possibly has biblical roots as Ecclesiastes 4:9-10 (AMP) speaks of the benefits of having the help of another person, especially when times are difficult and there is a risk of falling.

Two are better than one . . . for if they fall, the one will lift up his fellow.

At this time, it's not only your baby that needs comforting, you do too. Find a friend or family member (possibly someone who has been through the teething process with their own older children). Find someone you can lean on and talk to about what you are going through. Someone who will just listen and sympathise and maybe give you a hug.

Hugs are proven to reduce stress levels. Are you getting enough hugs?

 Prayer

Heavenly Father,

You are Almighty God, creator of heaven and earth. You made us in Your image. You designed every part of our development from cradle to grave, including teething.

Father, I know what is happening with my baby is a temporary stage. I thank You that there are so many pain-relief options available to help us to get through the teething process.

Please give me ideas as to which options to try and help me to find a solution that helps my baby. Please help me too, especially during the nights when I get less sleep and the days when my baby is irritable and unable to settle. Guide me to little things that restore me and uplift me.

Strengthen me and harden me to this difficulty. Give me peace in my heart even while there is little peace in my house.

I ask this in Jesus' name.

Thank you, Father,

Amen

Recommended song

"In My Arms" by Plumb

Written by: Tiffany Arbuckle Lee, Matt Bronleewe, Jeremy Bose

Plumb is the stage name for Tiffany Arbuckle who is another Christian singer, songwriter, performer with an impressive back catalogue of tracks across a wide variety of musical genres, including rock and electronic dance. This track is not overtly Christian in its lyrics but, as a mother, she captures the heartrending love that we feel for our little ones and the way in which, even during life's storms, we do our very best to offer them the love and safety they need. This song has a truly haunting melody that makes my eyes tear up whenever I hear it. If the frustrations of teething are driving you to the edge, I pray this track will bring you back and help you and your little one through.

Mum Memories

Suggestion

Your space to use as you choose.

How many baby teeth have already arrived? How many still to come? How will you celebrate once they are all through?

Guilty Mother Syndrome

Becoming a mother brings a multitude of emotions, mainly relief to be through childbirth and joy to finally meet your baby face to face, hold him or her in your arms and welcome them into your family.

There is so much to learn in the early days, especially for a first-time mum, and it seems being a parent is a continuous learning experience. I once heard that:

"Parenting is one glorious, messy experiment."

I couldn't agree more!

As we progress through the different tests that mothering brings we master some things quickly out of necessity, such as nappy changing, and find other skills take a bit longer before we feel competent, like dressing your tiny babe without bending their arms the wrong way as you put sleeves on, or trimming tiny finger nails and toe nails without nipping your child. And some skills we never master – making homemade organic baby food was never an option for me with my limited cooking skills and the supermarket baby aisle came to my rescue there.

There is one thing, however, that we mothers are all experts at immediately – self-assessment. We all have a voice in our head judging us and telling us how we've done. It's as though the birth of our child brings with it an app that automatically installs itself inside our head as the umbilical chord is cut and it's called Guilty Mother Syndrome. It lays

103

dormant waiting for triggers to come along then it springs into ugly action.

There are numerous triggers for this app and they differ mother to mother. I've mentioned homemade baby food. Another guilt trigger for me was cleaning my baby's first milk teeth. My daughter would not let me get anywhere close and I beat myself up so much about my dental-hygiene failure, convinced her beautiful little teeth would turn black and fall out due to my inability to clean them twice a day. Another of my triggers was whenever my child hurt herself. My daughter started rolling rather than crawling and one day, true to form, she rolled into the side of a cupboard in the lounge and gave herself a huge bruise on her forehead just 10 minutes before we had to leave for nursery. Oh, the horror! Oh, the shame! My Guilty Mother app sprang into action saying I had obviously neglected her and what would the nursery staff think of me?

Some triggers we share and others are individual to us, but the end result is the same – a feeling of self-condemnation for in some way being an inadequate parent. But this self-condemnation is not from God, and this is what we are discussing today.

One common trigger for Guilty Mother Syndrome is feeding formula milk to your baby instead of breastfeeding. This area is a minefield and I tread very carefully into it knowing I may be criticised and misunderstood, but I have met so many mothers who are burdened and tied up with guilt over having chosen or turned to formula that it is worth including here to shine a biblical perspective on the matter. At this point I will put on my spiritual armour, pick up my shield of faith and obediently keep going.

For mums who choose to breastfeed the level of support from midwives, health visitors and special baby groups is often high. It needed to be high for a hapless mum like me. I had no clue and such a big gap between my babies meant I needed teaching twice. I gave it my best shot for as long as I could and I'm glad I did. There were many wonderful, tender, peaceful feeds and the frequent night-time feeds were straightforward. However, it was not a bed of roses. Sore nipples, blocked milk ducts, mastitis, growth spurts and initial anxiety about feeding in public (not to mention in church) are also part and parcel of the breastfeeding experience for many mums, me included. Combine that with going back to work and it is a complex decision for many.

Most of us are helped to breastfeed if we want to and free to choose which option works best for us and our family.

But guilt can hang around the neck of a mum who chooses formula and this guilt is not from God.

God is not judging you for your choices or constantly assessing you on your performance as you learn to mother your baby.

He loves you very much. You are His child remember. As much as you love your baby, God feels even more deeply about you. Imagine!

Please be clear on the message here. It is not anti-breastfeeding. It is anti-unnecessary guilt tripping – whatever the trigger may be. Feeding decisions are a common cause of guilt for mothers and for me teeth cleaning, weaning and bumps and bruises were too. But

John 3:17 (NIV) reads:

For God did not send his Son into the world to condemn the world, but to save the world through him.

Jesus is more concerned about your soul and whether you believe in Him. There is a promise attached to doing this and it comes in the next part.

Verse 18 (AMP) says:

He who believes in Him [who clings to, trusts in, relies on Him] is not judged [. . . for him there is no rejection, no condemnation . . .]

Wow! How amazing! How freeing! No rejection and no condemnation.

That's not to say there is no correction. God will correct us but not through guilt and shame. So how do you move forward if you are weighed down with self-condemnation as you raise your baby?

Whatever the triggers are for your Guilty Mother Syndrome you can de-install the app.

In John 8:15 (AMP) Jesus says:

You [set yourself up to] judge according to the flesh (by what you see). [You condemn by external human standards.] I do not [set Myself up to] judge or condemn or sentence anyone.

Verse 31 and 32:

Jesus said to those . . . who had believed in Him, If you abide in My word [hold fast to My teachings and live in accordance with them], you are truly My disciples.

And you will know the Truth and the Truth will set you free.

You can access the Truth by aligning your thinking with the Bible. This is what "abide in My word and hold fast to My teachings" means. Know in your heart that you are not condemned by Jesus and make His opinion matter most in your life.

Praise God for your baby's health and growth.

Thank God if you live in a country where you have information, support and options.

Ask Him to give you perspective and balance and kindness in how you view yourself as a parent.

Trust Him to help you as you hold fast to His Word and let His Truth set you free.

I pray you be released, in Jesus' name, from the triggers that cause you to feel unnecessary guilt as a mother and that you be encouraged.

You are doing a great job! Be blessed x

 Putting it into practice

In the topic above I mentioned a few of my guilty mother triggers. Did any of them resonate with you? In order to put this into practice it will help if you first have a think about:

    a. What triggers make you feel like an inadequate mother?

b. When do these triggers occur?

c. Where do these triggers occur?

Do you know what your guilt triggers are? If you have clarity on your top 3 then write them down. For me my top 3 were:

1. My inability to brush Ania's milk teeth.

2. The bruises my daughter got from rolling around instead of crawling.

3. Giving my daughter supermarket baby food instead of making everything myself.

Getting a better idea of the "when" and "where" involves understanding the situations and circumstances that bring these self-condemnatory thoughts to the surface. If you know them then write that down too.

For me the places and timings were as follows:

Cleaning her teeth

Morning and evening in the bathroom I would try to brush her teeth and it was always a flashpoint of frustration. It didn't matter what type of brush I tried, nothing worked and it always put a dampener on the start of the day and especially bedtime.

Bumps and bruises

This would happen at total random so there was nothing I could identify as a regular place or time that would trigger it. But there was something about bumps happening just before we went out of the house that affected me more because the shame and guilt felt worse then. This was possibly because I imagined people were looking at Ania and judging me.

Feeding

When I went to do the weekly shopping at the supermarket and I was in the baby aisle, just being there, surrounded by food options would trigger my "why can't you make homemade food for your daughter?" accusations.

If you are struggling to recognise your specifics then consider perhaps the following:

- Do you know if there is a particular time of day / week / month that your guilt is triggered most often? When is it?

- Is there a person whose company tends to leave you feeling down on yourself?

- Are there activities you do with your baby that regularly leave you criticising yourself inwardly on how you handled it? Actually, for some mums going to church with their baby on Sunday can be a guilt trigger and that's why there is a topic for that all of its own later in this book.

Once you have a clearer idea of what these guilty mother triggers are and where and when they strike then you are in a better place to start to pray about them *before* you find yourself under attack.

God is not watching over you and tut-tutting. He is watching over you, ever-loving.

Prayer

Lord Jesus,

Thank You that You came to show me how much God loves me and that He doesn't want to judge me or condemn me but help me. Jesus, please help me to see that You are not keeping score on my performance as a mum, and neither is my heavenly Father.

I have heard the verse "the Truth will set you free" before and I would like to know the Truth and get this freedom. So often I have accusing thoughts telling me I am not good enough and I don't measure up as a mum.

Please help me to recognise and pray against my guilt triggers before they come up and learn to see them as nasty lies. The truth is that I am doing the best I can day by day. The truth is I am not perfect but with Your help I am good enough.

Thank You, Jesus,

Amen

 Recommended song

"Freedom" by Jesus Culture (New Song Café version)

Written by: Mia Fieldes, Kristian Stanfill, Brett Younker, Hank Bentley, Jordan Frye

Jesus Culture isn't the name of a group but of an organisation set up to bring the gospel to young people. It is another hugely successful outreach from Bethel Church in California. Kimberlee Walker Smith is the lead singer for this stripped-back acoustic guitar track, which is recorded live and performed in a relaxed sofa setting. Kimberlee urges us to embrace the grace that will release us from feeling trapped and weighed down. This is a wonderful example of weaving Bible verses into a modern song. There is power in singing these lyrics over our lives. When I listen to and watch this track, I can feel the Holy Spirit's healing vibe just cancelling out whatever lies have held me back. I pray you find Freedom when you listen too.

Mum Memories

Your space to use as you choose.

Suggestion

Have you ever de-installed an unwanted app on your mobile phone? It frees up valuable internal memory space for more useful things. How will you use your freed-up head space once you have de-installed the Guilty Mother app?

Toddler Section

Hurray! Your Bouncing Baby has become a Toddler! Welcome to the world of wilful energy, innocent curiosity, giggles and noisy tantrums. Jesus came that we might have life and have it in abundance. Our toddlers certainly have that!

As a toddler, my daughter learned to walk by holding both my forefingers as a support. I will never forget the backache I got from being stooped over to give my lovely girl confidence to keep walking.

Forever etched upon my memory are the endless times my toddler-aged son stopped on the pavement to crouch down and carefully explore snails, cigarette ends and discarded chewing gum. Once I'd coaxed him away his focus would switch immediately to playing the Up-the-doorstep and Down-the-doorstep game. As we walked very slowly, hand in hand, along the street not missing a single step, we were late for everything.

As our babies become little people with strong personalities, we need to change gear ourselves to keep up. For mums returning to work during this season it brings a whole new gamut of negative self-talk that needs rooting out.

The Toddler section addresses four more universal parenting struggles and gives you scripture to anchor yourself to when the waves start to rise. God's promises are reliable so together we can address each topic and replace the stormy waters within us for His peace and soul-deep calm.

As with all the other sections in this book, there are recommended songs to accompany each topic. The lyrics speak into each challenge with God's love and truth and have been hand-picked by me for you. I pray you find them to be a comfort and a source of godly strength.

Here are the topics covered and the recommended songs:

Starting Childcare

> Recommended song
> "Steady My Heart" by Kari Jobe

Baby Brain

> Recommended song
> "You Say" by Lauren Daigle

Small Children and Church

> Recommended song
> "Jesus Loves Me" by Listener Kids

When Patience Runs Out

> Recommended song
> "This Is The Stuff" by Francesca Battistelli

If you would like to see the short Toddler Intro video, please scan the QR code or follow the link below

https://mumschat.thinkific.com/courses/toddler-series

Starting Childcare

For many mums, especially those in the USA, going back to your career often comes long before your baby grows into a toddler. Many women only take a few months away after childbirth. However, in other parts of the world, such as the UK and Europe, maternity leave allows mums the option to take more time off and as a result babies are often much older when mum goes back to the world of work outside the home.

So, it was difficult for me to decide in which section this topic fit best. Infant, Bouncing Baby or Toddler. The more I thought about it the more I concluded that there isn't a right answer here so . . .

If you are a mum in the USA or another country where there is no lengthy maternity leave and you are returning to your job when your baby is very young, please know this section is equally relevant for you. I fully accept that, from your perspective, this topic is in the wrong age section.

However, the spiritual and practical suggestions apply regardless of the age of your baby and I hope you can understand my dilemma in where to place this subject in the book. Equally, I hope you will bear with me with grace when I talk about maternity leave, especially if you never had any. I'm confident the content will be helpful to you anyway. Are we all on the same page? Yes? Thank you. Ok, here we go . . .

Going back to your job after maternity leave can create feelings of fear and dread, especially for a first-time mum. In my work as a maternity coach, I address this with every client to help them to understand the process, plan effectively and turn the dread into positive anticipation. But dread seems to be the main emotion we mums feel initially at the thought of leaving our baby with a childcare provider – even if that person is a family member.

It's normal and we see it replicated in the animal kingdom with cows bellowing when separated from their calves and bitches howling when their puppies are taken away by new owners.

It's no surprise, then, that starting childcare can be tricky for both mum and baby. I refer to this phenomenon as separation tolerance. That is a mum's ability to tolerate being separated from her baby. This is something that increases with practice, like a muscle forming due to exercise. It certainly isn't something a mother finds easy to start with. Dread can loom large and anxiety can creep in. How will your baby settle in their new routine without you? How will you cope without them?

The good news is that your separation tolerance can be built up before you go back to work but only by regularly being apart from your baby and for increasing periods of time. Maybe you can approach this with your childcare provider and arrange a staged introduction to childcare. This will be as much for your benefit as for your baby. This usually helps a great deal and makes the first day back at work less of a shock to the system for both of you. There are multiple benefits:

- you are more practised in terms of preparation at home in the morning,

- you are more aware of the journey and how rush-hour traffic might affect your timings,

- and very importantly you and your baby are more used to that moment of goodbye – the childcare hand over – even if that still involves tears on both sides.

Two mothers in the Bible experienced very extreme handovers to childcare providers. These childcare providers would offer permanent new homes for their babies.

In Exodus chapter 2 we read about the infant Moses. His mother, Jochebed, must have been full of so many emotions as she laid her beautiful 3-month-old baby boy into a waterproofed basket in the bulrushes of the River Nile. She had very little alternative as the Egyptian Pharaoh had instructed all newborn Israelite boys be killed to instil population control among his slaves.

What a truly horrific situation to be in as a parent. Jochebed was between a rock and a hard place. I absolutely cannot imagine kissing my baby, for what may be the last time, laying him or her gently into a floating basket and pushing them away from reach into one of the biggest rivers in the world.

But Jochebed had faith and godly wisdom and she tasked her older daughter, Miriam, to keep an eye on the little basket and its precious contents. From a distance her daughter saw what happened next. Moses was found in the bulrushes by Pharaoh's own daughter as she went to bathe in the Nile with her entourage.

She must have known she had found a Hebrew baby and she would have known her father's murderous decree too, but she rescued this little baby anyway. Moses was saved and raised in a palace with his birth mother as his wet nurse until he was weaned.

The second story is in 1 Samuel chapters 1 and 2 where we learn that a godly woman named Hannah longed to be a mother but she was seemingly infertile and her inability to have children brought her great suffering. In Old Testament times there was a great stigma attached to wives who could not give their husband a child, so her suffering would have been both private and public.

Yet when her prayer was answered and she had a baby boy she told her husband that as soon as Samuel was weaned he would be entrusted to the Lord's service at the temple, many miles away, to thank God for his faithfulness.

That meant Hannah was entrusting Samuel's life to the priest Eli permanently when Samuel was very small indeed. She wouldn't see him learn to walk and talk. She wouldn't be there for birthdays. At that stage in her life Hannah had no idea whether she would have any more children and she knew she would only get to see Samuel once every year after he had been handed over.

Despite all this Hannah was determined to dedicate her son to God's service in gratitude and God must have put that decision and determination in her heart because Samuel needed special spiritual training for the role God had in store in his future.

Putting it into practice

Thankfully none of you will be handing your baby to another person to raise on a permanent basis – you are simply going back to the world of work outside the home. But we can learn from something else that these stories have in common.

1) Entrusting your little one to Him

Both of these mothers were godly women and, as such, before they handed their children over in the physical sense, they would have first handed them over to God in the spiritual sense, entrusting their precious sons to God's protection and having faith that God would honour them and ensure His plan for their baby's life came about. And we can do the same. We can entrust our children to God's care in our absence and pray for wisdom and blessings upon those who will be caring for our children while we are away. Doing this in conjunction with building your separation tolerance will combine into a winning strategy.

2) Know that God has a plan for your child

To help you as you face this new experience remember that God knows the end from the beginning for us and our children and He loves your child more than even you do. He wants to guide your child's future and has been taking a watchful interest in them from the start.

In Isaiah 41:4 (AMP) Gods says:

Who has prepared and done this, calling forth and guiding the destinies of the generations . . . from the beginning? I, the Lord – the first . . . and with the last . . . I am He.

3) Ask to be strengthened and hardened to the task

A few verses later in Isaiah 41:10 (AMP) He speaks to a mother's heart again:

Fear not [there is nothing to fear], for I am with you; do not look around you in terror and be dismayed, for I am your God. I will strengthen and harden you to difficulties, yes, I will help you; yes, I will hold you up and retain you with My [victorious] right hand of rightness and justice.

God hardened Jochebed to her difficulty and enabled her to put her baby into the basket on the river. God made Hannah determined to dedicate her first-born son to God's temple and go through with it. He was in control of Moses' and Samuel's destiny, and He is in control of your child's destiny too. He will give you the strength to hand your child over, entrusted both to Him and your childcare provider.

4) Get closure on this special season as it draws to an end

As this precious time of being at home 24/7 with your baby draws to an end think how you can celebrate, capture and get closure before you move into this next phase of life.

It doesn't have to be complicated or extravagant. It might be a picnic in the park. Maybe it's a baby's first day at childcare photo or something else entirely. You've come such a long way in a very short time. Capture it, celebrate it, get closure on it.

5) Let Him comfort you as you walk away

Further on in Isaiah 66 there is a wonderful series of verses alluding to childbirth and breastfeeding, and in verse 13 (NIV) it reads:

As a mother comforts her child, so I will comfort you; and you will be comforted.

So, as you kiss your child goodbye, say a prayer over them and their carer. Turn around and leave resolutely and make your way to work knowing that your little one has a destiny that God has already planned. They are safe in His care. You are strengthened and helped to go your separate ways for the day. Right now, while this is still new – it's ok to cry.

Waterproof mascara is a wonderful going-back-to-work investment. It will get easier as time goes on. Your tolerance will grow and you will harden. Once you get to your place of work, a quick phone call to your childcare provider will reassure you that your baby has already settled and is getting on with their day – so you can feel free to get on with yours.

Saying goodbye can be equally challenging as children grow and go to school. My parting words every morning at primary school have been the same prayer-based blessing:

"God bless you and keep you safe, have fun and be good for your teacher."

It's the same words or similar every morning along with a kiss and a hug, regardless of who is watching or listening.

It is our moment. Perhaps you can think of something you can say as you part. A short prayer of blessing that feels right for you both, that allows God into your goodbye. A brief sentence that becomes knitted into your routine, a godly habit, a tender moment of dedication that seals your parting with God's protection and gives you peace as you leave.

It's amazing how a one-line prayer, said at the right time, can steady and strengthen you.

 Prayer

Heavenly Father,

Thank You that I have found childcare for my child before I go back to my job. Thank You for helping me through that process.

Despite making the best decision I can, I still feel a looming dread and a sadness at the thought of leaving my precious little one with someone else.

Heavenly Father, You know what it is to entrust Your child to the care of someone else. You entrusted Your only Son Jesus, as an infant, to the care of Mary and Joseph. You let Him leave You in heaven to fulfil His mission. You let Him go and You watched over Him closely.

Heavenly Father, please comfort me in the first few days and weeks and harden me to the "goodbye" moment. Help me to find positive parting words of blessing to bring You into that moment. To bless my childcare provider too.

Fill my heart with Your peace and Your calm, even if my baby and I both cry. Help me through the sadness as I walk away and help me not to look back. Help me to know we are both in Your hands despite being apart and this separation is part of Your plan for our growth.

In Jesus' name I ask,

Amen

 Recommended song

"Steady My Heart" by Kari Jobe

Written by: Matt Bronleewe, Ben Glover, Kari Jobe

I chose this song because starting childcare was an emotionally wobbly moment for me. At that time I didn't even know about separation tolerance and, looking back, I recognise mine was woefully low. No one explained that building this up would make the handover process easier. As a result, when I went back to my career, starting childcare was like taking an emotional cold shower every morning.

I was under prepared. I felt guilty, deeply sad and I cried . . . a lot. This song, whenever I listen to it, does exactly what the title suggests. The lines in the chorus, and the soulful way Kari sings them, capture exactly how I felt as I made my way to the office after saying goodbye to my little one at nursery. But by the time I hear the final three lines of "Steady My Heart" I'm always in a far better place. I hope it helps you too.

Mum Memories

Suggestion

Your space to use as you choose.

As this precious time of being at home 24/7 draws to an end how can you capture it, celebrate it, get closure on it?

Baby Brain

"Baby what?" I hear some of you say.

Well, I came across the term Baby Brain during my first maternity leave. The mums in my mother and baby group used to refer to it regularly. They used it to describe several things including:

- a feeling of fuzzy headedness,

- forgetfulness,

- clumsiness and

- a sort of mental paralysis.

I'm sure you can relate to that sensation of starting a sentence but forgetting a word in the middle and then losing your thread completely. We've all been there.

In my work as a maternity coach, I describe Baby Brain as reduced personal effectiveness and lowered self-confidence. This is something that all mums talk about during coaching, with lowered professional self-confidence regularly coming up in sessions as I help clients prepare to return to work, whenever that time comes.

Another quick side note here: I appreciate that returning to work often comes a lot earlier than the toddler stage for many mums, especially for those who don't have maternity leave. Just like the previous topic, this subject is tricky to put an exact time to in terms of child development.

I am confident the content here will be just as relevant to you however long or short your time away from your job has been and whether or not you are returning to the world of work outside the home or staying at home (which is definitely also work).

Baby Brain bites regardless. Please know there is benefit for you in these pages regardless of how young or old your child is. Thank you for your understanding in my topic placement dilemma. Are we good to go? Ok, let's get back to it . . .

For many mums it's as though becoming a parent has sabotaged our ability to be whatever we were before our baby arrived. Many women today have enjoyed a career before becoming a parent and completed some form of training or education to carry out their job. Looking after a baby rarely requires you to draw upon your professional abilities and it can feel as though this part of your mental capability has ground to a halt and is gathering dust and cobwebs.

Whether you are going back to the world of paid work after having your baby or staying at home to work as a full-time mum, none of us needs Baby Brain and its confidence-squashing side effects.

To start with we'll look at the circumstances, during your time away from work, that can allow Baby Brain to take hold and how Baby Brain can lead to lowered confidence. Then we'll look at some Baby Brain busting Bible verses and a couple of maternity coaching techniques to help you to overcome this phenomenon whether you are going back to your career or working at home as a full-time mum.

So firstly, let's take a snapshot look at your morning routine before your baby arrived and then fast forward to your morning routine now that baby is on the scene.

Before your baby was born your morning may have looked something like this:

* Wake up refreshed after a continuous 8 hours of sleep.

* Shower and get dressed for work.

* Select accessories to complement your outfit, possibly spritz perfume, do your make-up and hair.

* Eat a prompt, uninterrupted breakfast.

* Grab handbag, phone and keys.

* Go to work remembering you have a dental appointment tomorrow.

* Feel organised and well-presented.

* Arrive at work and contribute in a meaningful way using your education, skills and experience.

Now your baby has arrived and you are at home being mum your day maybe looks more like this:

* Wake up after an inadequate, disrupted sleep feeling fuzzy headed.

* Feed, change and dress your baby. Change baby's nappy again 5 minutes later.

* Eat breakfast one handed whilst holding baby.

* Secure your comforted baby in a play pen or baby

rocker and take a short shower enjoying the only "me time" you will get all day.

* Dry hair, sort of style it and hope for the best (note: accessories, perfume and make-up are rarely part of your routine these days).

* Put on clothes that sort of fit and are sort of clean (note that ironing clothes is a thing of the past).

* Spend 30 minutes gathering the mass of items required to leave the house.

* Realise your dental appointment was yesterday.

* Arrive at your mother and baby group 15 minutes late and talk about celebrity gossip and the challenges of motherhood.

Clearly life has changed!

And even though I know you wouldn't change you new life for the world, when you see how radically different it is now it's easy to understand how Baby Brain can take hold.

- You have less rest which affects your mental capacity.

- You have less control over your time and how you spend it.

- You have less stimulation from varied conversation with other adults.

- You have virtually no time for yourself.

- You are disconnected from your job, which was possibly the part of your life that previously gave you purpose, recognition and reward.

Now your purpose and reward come from being a mum to your child and although they are lovely, they can't tell you what a great job you are doing when things get tough.

So that leaves the little voice in your head opportunity to pipe up and tell you that you've lost your edge and you will never recover it.

For the woman who has decided to work as a stay-at-home mum that voice might say:

"If you can't even remember what you came into the kitchen for how are you going to run a home effectively?"

For the mum who has decided to go back to their career soon the voice might say:

"If you keep forgetting words in the middle of speaking, how are you going to cope in meetings at work?"

Our inner-self shrinks when we feel our confidence getting a battering.

"You don't make the grade anymore"

is the message in your head every time you forget something or get muddled or clumsy.

Well, the Bible has plenty to offer mums who feel they have reduced self-confidence and personal effectiveness. Let's take a look at some Baby Brain busting Bible verses.

Psalm 25 seems to speak directly to a mum going back to her career after maternity leave. I remember exactly how I felt myself in my first few days and weeks as I went back to my job. At that time, I wasn't a maternity coach. I worked in a global organisation and my job involved regular foreign travel, lots of meetings, creating reports and managing a team. I was deeply worried that, when I returned to work, I would have nothing to contribute because my brain was out of gear and stuck in neutral. Basically, I couldn't remember my job.

Psalm 25:20-21 (AMP) says:

> O keep me, Lord, and deliver me; let me not be ashamed or disappointed, for my trust and my refuge are in You.
>
> Let integrity and uprightness preserve me, for I wait for and expect You.

If this strikes a chord with you then maybe you can re-read this verse, add some tailoring and turn it into a Baby Brain busting prayer. Note the words in *italics* are added by me for a mum going back to her career.

> O keep me, Lord, and deliver me; let me not be ashamed or disappointed *in myself,*
>
> for my trust and my refuge are in You *so I'll keep quiet for now and listen to everyone else in these meetings as I catch up.*
>
> Let integrity and uprightness preserve me *as I get to grips with my job all over again.*
>
> for I wait for and expect You *to restore my confidence and my professional capability.*
>
> Amen

Obviously, for a mum who has decided to work as a stay-at-home mum the words will need to be slightly different and tailored to your role as a home manager. Something like this might be more suitable:

> O keep me, Lord, and deliver me; let me not be ashamed or disappointed *in myself,*

> for my trust and my refuge are in You *so I'll keep calm and listen for Your quiet small voice to guide me in all I do at home today.*

> Let integrity and uprightness preserve me *as I make daily decisions for my family,*

> for I wait for and expect You *to restore my confidence and build my home management capability.*

> Amen

 Putting it into practice

To finish this *Mums Chat* topic there is another psalm I want to share with you but, before I do, I did promise to let you in on some helpful maternity coaching techniques too – so here they are.

These are two practical steps that I recommend to all mothers regardless of whether you are planning to go back to paid employment or whether you decide instead to work as a full-time mum in your home. You can do them before your baby arrives or after baby has arrived, it doesn't matter – the value is still there.

1) Dust off your CV / resume and make it shine

The first is to make sure your CV or resume is up to date regardless of whether you think you will need it in the near future or not. It's surprising how quickly we all forget our work-based achievements and contributions. When you pick up this document in the future your confidence will surely be boosted by reminding yourself of what you have accomplished, with the Lord's help.

2) Create a career-focused pre-baby time capsule

My second recommendation is to create something like a time capsule of what the world looked like in your company, in your job or career or industry before your baby arrived. This could include a copy of your job description, most recent evaluation / performance appraisal, any objectives that were set for you and your team, organisation charts, project plans, competitor activity and industry developments, etc.

Basically, include whatever you think captures your job, organisation, etc. at the point at which you left to have your baby. You could even include a copy of a daily newspaper or a favourite magazine. That might well make you smile later.

This will be so useful as and when and if you go back and need to reconnect. Just looking at this pack will help you to re-engage with your workplace. It will also enable your colleagues to help you to fill in the gaps and get you back up to speed.

Often, bosses and colleagues forget that you've been away and assume you understand the background to things that happened during your absence. Creating a career-focused pre-baby time capsule shows them clearly what the state of play was when you left and where they need to update you on what has happened since. It's very simple to do and everyone wins.

Equally, if you plan to work as a stay-at-home mum, this info pack will help remind you of the role you left (and maybe why you left it). Even if you have no plan to return to the same sort of work it will help you to reconnect with the personal skills you needed then and still have to offer now. You never know what the future holds and having this info kept aside will be such a boost if you need to use it, at a later date, to return to the world of paid work.

These are two small but significant practical steps you can take to combat reduced confidence and remind yourself of your achievements whenever you need to.

3) Take the focus off yourself and put your confidence in Him

The final psalm we will look at for this topic is Psalm 71:1, 5, 6 and 8 (AMP). Again, it could have been written for us mums in this situation.

In You, O Lord, do I put my trust and confidently take refuge; let me never be put to shame or confusion!

For You are my hope; O Lord God, You are my trust from my youth and the source of my confidence.

Upon You have I leaned and relied from birth; You are He Who took me from my mother's womb and You have been my benefactor from that day. My praise is continually of You.

My mouth shall be filled with Your praise and with Your honour all the day.

When we take the focus off ourselves and focus on our confidence being rooted in Him that's when we can exhale, relax, shift the burden onto Him and give Him the space to step into our situation and do something amazing.

Baby Brain is a very real phenomenon – our personal and professional self-confidence can take a battering whilst we are focused on baby raising. Every client I have ever worked with has found returning to their career tricky to start with; however, their confidence was restored after a few months.

Your previous education, skills and experience are all still intact and just waiting to be reactivated however, whenever and wherever you choose to use them.

Trust Him to restore you and be blessed – you are still brilliant x

 Prayer

Heavenly Father,

Thank You so much for Psalm 25 and 71. These words encourage me to put myself into Your hands and trust You as I go forward.

Please help me as I take this next step because it feels quite stressful and I feel vulnerable. My confidence in myself is not where it used to be. I need to rely on You for calm as I find my feet. I may need to rediscover skills I haven't used for a while. I may need to develop new skills.

Please give me wisdom as I settle into a new routine, give me the confidence to do my best each day, to contribute positively in my work setting and please help me to be kind to myself as I grow.

Thank You that You are trustworthy, You are with me and You won't fail me.

In Jesus' name I ask,

Amen

 Recommended song

"You Say" by Lauren Daigle

Written by: Bebo Norman, Jason Ingram, Michael Donehey, Paul Mabury, Lauren Daigle

What can I say about Lauren Daigle? Multi-award-winning singer and songwriter, for me she is the Christian world's equivalent of Adele. I do hope that comment is taken as the compliment it is intended to be. In fact, when I first heard her sing, I thought I was listening to Adele. Lauren's voice is captivating. A truly world-class performer, her tracks are of a quality both in terms of lyrics and musical composition that just set her apart. If you have never encountered her work before, it is a treasure to be discovered.

This track is perfect for this topic of Baby Brain when all we hear are voices of negativity and we wonder if we can re-integrate back into our careers or become the capable Proverbs 31-type home manager.

Lauren reminds us that it is what God says about us that matters most and she enables us to sing positivity over ourselves in the depths of negativity. This song will firstly cradle you, then pick you up and get you back on your feet fighting. Starting with a simple piano chord and building to a gospel choir-backed, string-enhanced track with so many layers this is a joy to listen to. It's time to banish Baby Brain.

Mum Memories

Your space to use as you choose.

Suggestion

Maybe leave this space blank for now and use it to write down your own Baby Brain Breakthrough example(s). I got my Baby Brain Breakthrough in a group meeting a few weeks after I'd been back at work. It was a great moment for me. I felt I was back in the saddle. You will have your breakthrough(s) too.

Small Children and Church

I can imagine that a few of you are already smiling or possibly recoiling and shrinking in embarrassment before I've even gotten started on this topic.

Taking babies and small children to church is something that must be experienced to be understood. For me it was the one time in the week that I used to really hope and pray that my baby slept through and my young child sat still. Sometimes they did but mostly they didn't.

Before you had children, going to church was probably exactly what you needed it to be. Perhaps it was a serene, peaceful, calming, holy opportunity to connect quietly with God, or perhaps an uplifting, joyful, re-energising spiritual boost where you worshipped with abandon and got lost in the praise.

But now it is often a tense, uncomfortable exercise in keeping your children as quiet as possible whilst you (breast)feed your baby, wipe your toddler's nose, provide a buffet of quiet, non-messy snacks and non-spill drinks, turn the pages of cardboard books and pick up dropped toys and crayons from underneath the chairs or pews in front of you.

Whilst you are seated the situation is sort of contained. There are ever-present dangers, such as preventing your toddler from wandering off to explore the altar and stopping your curious bouncing baby from grabbing the clothing of the person sitting in front of you. However, once you are all up on your feet, navigating your family safely to the front of the church for communion is like herding cats and has a high level of unpredictability.

Churches vary with huge differences in terms of family-friendly facilities. Each church has its small child magnets. Whichever church you go to there are quiet times of reverence during the service and items and places of holy significance for which young children have no understanding what-so-ever and total disregard.

Some churches have pretty flowers that toddlers find irresistible.

Some churches have altar steps and we all know about young children and the Up-the-step and Down-the-step game.

Some churches have easy-to-reach candles that are lit during the service.

When you combine all of these elements you find yourself in a supremely stressful environment. Basically, going to church with babies and small children can be a Code Red High Alert situation for mums and dads. It's no wonder so many parents find it a very tricky time.

I have various memories of my daughter as a pre-schooler doing un-church-like things in church. Spilling snacks happened often. Thankfully, banging her head on the wooden pew and wailing with the pain happened less often. Getting thoroughly fed up and asking in a very loud, bored voice, "Can we go home now?" was an awkward phase we went through too.

But none of this is unusual behaviour for little ones. Sometimes little kids being little kids in church is just a joy. I remember when she was still at the age where she loved to dress up and she insisted on going to church one Palm Sunday wearing her Nativity donkey costume.

I saw the relevance immediately. Didn't Jesus enter Jerusalem riding on a donkey? She had no knowledge of this of course. It was just what she had decided to wear that day, but she melted hearts that Sunday. Her unwitting contribution to the service was very well received.

Equally, whilst my son was a pre-schooler, his contribution was less of a joy for his Sunday school teacher. I vividly recall a conversation they had where his teacher was trying to teach the children about generosity and how it can be a gift to others. Daniel had lots of energy and he rarely sat down with the other children on the mat. At his tender age he had no awareness that he was expected to put his hand up and be chosen to offer his answer, so despite my attempts, he was busy wandering around the room shouting out his valuable contributions.

His Sunday school teacher asked, "Do presents have to be big?"

"Yes!" shouted my son.

"Err no, they don't," she replied, glancing in his direction.

She continued, "Do presents have to be expensive?"

"Yes!" shouted my son, again super pleased with his clearly correct answer.

She smiled sweetly and said, "No, they don't."

She continued, "If you have some toys and you don't want them anymore what could you do with them?"

Of course, she was angling at being thoughtful and kind and giving them to someone in need. But before anyone else could say anything my son, who was clearly on a roll by this point, piped up,

"Put them in the bin!"

She rose above his innocent heckling and continued.

"Well, no, you could give them to a baby or another child maybe?" she offered fixing her eyes on him.

My son had clearly had enough at this point as his valuable contributions were not being appreciated. He proclaimed loudly to the class,

"Mummy, I need the toilet!"

And so we have yet another Sunday school success story. I had to just chalk it up to experience because he wasn't being naughty; he was just saying what he thought was a good answer unaware of social norms and etiquette. Thankfully, he has learned a bit more decorum since then.

And it's not only children that are on a steep learning curve when we go to church – us parents are too. We soon learn where to park the pram, which non-messy snacks to bring and in which easy-and-quiet-to-open containers, which drip-safe bottles work best and which silent toys will entertain the children but not interrupt the service. But we learn by trial and error.

One particularly memorable learning moment for me was when my daughter brought her Jesse doll from *Toy Story* to church. Do your children have a pull-string toy like this? As the priest blessed the bread and wine for communion my daughter pulled the doll's string and by then it was too late. Among the reverent silence and bowed heads everyone heard, "Yee Hah!"

Children are children. They are very good at it. Sadly, many of my friends stopped coming to church because they felt their children's behaviour would be frowned upon or ruin the service for others or that it was too stressful to be restraining their child for the duration.

It is true there have been moments when I was sure I could feel disapproving eyes burning into the back of my neck and people in front have turned around to look behind them to see where the noise is coming from. Managing babies and small children in a Sunday service is not easy.

Equally, I'm sure I also made assumptions about other people's opinions and judgements that may have been incorrect. And in truth it is only God's opinion of us that matters. That is what we should hold most dear. So, we are going to look at two questions:

- How can you navigate this difficult terrain?

and

- What does God say in His Word about babies and small children?

143

Putting it into practice

Navigating this terrain is easier if you consider the practical things you can do to make the experience better for you, your family and your church.

1) Ask other parents about facilities and unspoken parenting protocols

I would definitely recommend that you talk to other mums and dads to find out whether there is a particular service for young families and what facilities and unspoken protocols exist. For example:

- Ask where to park the pram.

- Ask whether there are any baby-change facilities and, if not, what do other parents do when the need arises?

- Is there a separate breastfeeding area or are you able to just get on with it in situ?

- Does the church have any toy boxes or puzzle books at the back?

Some family-focused churches have a glass-fronted room near the main service where you can take your noisy little one and still hear and see the service being piped through to you. I've used one of these and it was wonderful.

2) Go and have a chat with your church leader

This practical suggestion seems obvious but so many parents don't do it. Instead, they sit uncomfortably during church wondering what other people are thinking about their noisy kids without actually finding out.

You will know immediately that your church leader really has a heart for families and I'm sure you will be reassured by their pragmatism and tolerance. When my children were simultaneously at the tiny baby and small child stage we were attending a Catholic church in a building with no family-friendly facilities at all. It didn't even have a nappy-change station, but the priest wasn't at all fazed by my children and was glad they were in church on Sunday morning. He said:

> *"Little ones moving around during the service is fine if it keeps them quiet as long as they are not wandering without supervision during communion, so no one gets tripped up."*

He was equally reassuring when I'd gone to him to ask about the breastfeeding-in-church dilemma and his answer at that time was emphatic. He raised his eyes and his hands to heaven and exclaimed in his lovely Irish brogue:

> *"How do you suppose that Mary fed our good Lord? Of course, breastfeeding in church is ok."*

A family service is for families and some noise and mess are to be expected. How are churches going to maintain or grow attendance levels if children are not welcome? The truth is children are welcome. Every minister, priest and vicar I've spoken with says the same thing:

> *"Come along and bring your children too. We have a family service for families."*

So, we've looked at a couple of practical suggestions for making the experience easier but what does God's Word say on the topic?

1) Children are not just welcome; they are the role models for adults

When I was looking up verses for this topic, I noticed something interesting that made it clear that children are welcome in church. In Matthew 19:13-14 (AMP) it reads:

> Then little children were brought to Jesus that He might put His hands on them and pray; but the disciples rebuked the parents who brought them.

> But He said, Leave the children alone! Allow the little ones to come to Me and do not forbid or restrain or hinder them, for of such [as these] is the kingdom of heaven composed.

At that time children were not seen in society as equal to adults. Jesus took the opportunity to explain that actually the adults needed to become more like children to enter heaven. That would have been quite a sobering revelation and it speaks very clearly to anyone who, like the disciples, might want to keep Jesus to themselves and create a holy in-crowd. Jesus didn't want an adult clique then and He doesn't want it now either. Our children are welcome.

2) Suffer little children

In the King James Version of the Bible the verse above, Matthew 19:14 says:

> Suffer little children, and forbid them not.

I really like this older version and although I am advised that "suffer" means to permit or tolerate, I honestly do feel there is an element of suffering too! I'm sure you will agree.

Furthermore, unless we "suffer little children" how will they know about our faith? How else will we pass it on? How will they know they are part of a wider church family?

After another fraught service (with an incident I won't divulge) a kind, older lady came up to me as I was gathering our scattered belongings off the floor and she smiled and said:

"Your children are lovely!"

"Thank you," I replied, feeling rather defeated. "But I'm not sure they are always lovely. They don't always behave very well. I think some people disapprove."

She responded instantly, "Well this is God's house and no one else's and He says your children are welcome."

That was a really enlightening moment for me. She was absolutely right. It didn't mean I could let my children run riot but kids being kids in a family service is fine.

3) Spiritual feeding and spiritual forming

In closing I'll share a wonderfully apt proverb that adds further to God's view on this topic.

Proverbs 22:6 (NKJV):

> Train up a child in the way he should go, and when he is old he will not depart from it.

It's never too early or too late to start the adventure that is bringing babies and young children to church. Remember it is God's house first and foremost; your children are welcome and they belong there just as much as anyone else. And despite your best efforts on the day – they will be children.

Ultimately, if you find it really isn't working, then it might be better to look for a church where the facilities, layout, service timings, etc., better meet this season of your life. Please don't stop going to church. Every Sunday matters and you need spiritual feeding as much as your child needs spiritual forming.

Be blessed as you do this hugely significant role-modelling and smile – because Jesus certainly will be.

 Prayer

Lord Jesus,

Thank You for the Bible verses that show me how important babies and small children are to both You and Your Father in heaven. Thank You for making a point of drawing these little ones to You in front of Your disciples to make it clear to everyone that they are equally valuable, equally loved.

Thank You for telling parents it was ok to bring their babies to You for a blessing. Thank You for making time and space for parents with little ones to come close.

I have read about You being the Good Shepherd who protects both His sheep and His lambs. A flock cannot be maintained or increase unless the young lambs are nurtured to become healthy full-grown sheep. And a new lamb needs to see the shepherd and get to know his voice just the same as an older sheep. I know I need to take my small children to church to meet You in Your Father's house and get to know You, but it can be hard.

Please give me wisdom, patience and a godly sense of humour as I go through this season. Hold me up as the toys fall down. Comfort me when it gets messy. Strengthen me to difficulties when it gets noisy. Wrap me up in Your love when I maybe don't "feel-the-love" from other church members.

I know that every visit to church as a family is time well invested and if I train up my child in the way they should go, then they will not depart from it when they are older.

Jesus, help me to smile and laugh the same way that You do as You watch it all unfold in Your Father's house. Let me hear You say a big, "Well done!" after each Sunday service and know You are by my side as I carry out this extremely important part of parenting.

Thank You, Lord,

Amen

 Recommended song

"Jesus Loves Me" by the Listener Kids

Written by: Peggy Duquesnel

This version of a much-loved traditional song is beautifully sung by little children. It is a classic Sunday school song that you might have sung yourself in the past. I certainly remember singing it and it reminds me of how it felt to be a child in church. This song also brings the Bible verses to life and affirms that Jesus loves our kids and accepts them. We all belong in church.

Mum Memories

Your space to use as you choose.

Suggestion

God has a sense of humour. He smiles and He laughs. He invented play. We know this because He created us in His image. He really enjoys seeing your little children in His house. How might this help you next Sunday morning?

When Patience Runs Out

When your patience runs out what runs in?

Do you ever lose your patience with your small child(ren)?

I suspect the answer is a great big Yes. I know I do . . . frequently!

When I think of my own capacity for patience, I imagine a new candle that is lit early each morning as I wake up and burns down during the day until by early evening there is very little candle left. My patience has almost run out. I used to joke that I prayed to God for patience and His answer was to send me my husband and children. Patience is one of those qualities that develop under pressure. It is not a pretty process and I am very much a work in progress in this area.

When my daughter was born a common trigger for losing my patience was trying to get us both out of the house to do something or go somewhere. I'm sure you know just what I mean. Once your baby arrives gone are the days when you grab your purse, your phone and your keys and set off.

Now you need to ensure you are ready for every conceivable situation and in the early days it requires a pram, nappies, wipes, nappy sacks, toys, a change of clothes for your child, nappy rash cream, baby food and, oh yes, your purse, phone and keys. It's much the same when they are pre-schoolers. You still need a long list of things whenever you leave the house and that might include a favourite toy, clean underwear, spare clothes, nappy sacks to bring soiled clothes home, a snack and a water bottle.

As if this wasn't enough there are those memorable days when – just as you are ready and about to leave the house – your baby does a poo or your pre-schooler has a "little accident" and you know your schedule is blown before you start.

It's back upstairs to change a nappy or wet clothes, not forgetting to put any poo-stained clothes to soak before you go out. Well, that is if you managed to clear the sink of dirty dishes earlier. Jobs back up behind each other as you respond to the next schedule-shattering event.

It's no wonder it takes massive effort to get the minimum done. It's no wonder we mums feel frazzled. You are not in complete control of your time anymore. Your priorities and plans are swept aside as you respond to the immediate needs of your child / children. And this is how your day plays out, every day.

And when patience runs out frustration and anger often run straight in.

I now have two children and it's even trickier. Trying to persuade my daughter to hurry up whilst simultaneously readying myself and my son to go out seems to require the most incredible amounts of preparation, negotiation and patience.

I have to admit there have been plenty of times when I have resorted to shouting, threatening and sometimes bodily carrying both children out to the car to strap them in. Then I jump into the driver's seat fuming while the kids complain noisily in the back. Hardly a recipe for peace and harmony! Hardly a Spirit-filled life. Sound familiar?

So as your patience runs out how can you stop anger and frustration running in?

  Putting it into practice

There are three short verses in particular that I turn to when I realise I'm at the end of my tether.

Psalm 28:7 (AMP):

> The Lord is my Strength and my . . . Shield; my heart trusts in . . . Him, and I am helped.

Proverbs 18:10 (NKJV):

> The name of the Lord is a strong tower; the righteous run to it and are safe.

Philippians 4:13 (NKJV):

> I can do all things through Christ who strengthens me.

These verses are powerful for a number of reasons.

1) Firstly, let's look at Psalm 28:7

> The Lord is my Strength and my . . . Shield; my heart trusts in . . . Him, and I am helped.

This is a recognition that we can't manage on our own. We need to call on God and ask Him for His strength and protection.

His shield is available to us if we ask for it and it will protect us from being injured by whatever is bombarding us – be it the relentless demands of our kids or the frequent schedule-busting events that often derail our plans when we are caring for our children.

But we have to decide to put our trust in Him and hand the situation over to Him. We have to hold our hands up and admit that we are out of steam on this one. In my case, when I use this verse, I usually say it out loud and very quickly. It's a genuine cry for help and I just need to get it out there. Try it yourself at your top tongue-twister speed:

"The-Lord-is-my-Strength-and-my-Shield-my-heart-trusts-in-Him-and-I'm-helped."

Then I say it again more slowly and I start to feel calmed and soothed. My breathing slows and deepens. I say it again, very deliberately, and put the emphasis wherever I need it to be at that moment.

"The Lord is MY Strength and MY Shield, my heart trusts in Him and I AM HELPED!"

I can regain my composure. I can start again. As the verse says – I am helped. And that often involves a bit of self-reflection and, at times, apologising to my children for my behaviour. The sweetest words I hear some days, from the back seat of my car, are "Mummy, I forgive you."

2) Let's look at the second verse

Proverbs 18:10 says:

> The name of the Lord is a strong tower; the righteous run to it and are safe.

This is so useful when I am tired, hungry and frustrated. You know the feeling. You've made it through till the children's bedtime and now they won't go to bed or go to sleep. This is supposed to be *your* precious time now and you are longing for a hot meal where you can sit down and not get up half a dozen times, just some peace and maybe a chat with your other half – but no. The demands from your children keep coming. In this situation I try to stop and just give myself a few moments downstairs with this verse.

> The name of the Lord is a strong tower. The righteous run to it and are safe.

And I close my eyes and I imagine that tower. Maybe you can do the same. I wonder what your tower will look like. My tower stands alone in the countryside on a grassy hill. My tower is very old and round, made of stone and is tall with thick walls that block the noise. I can run inside where it is cool, quiet and safe and close the door behind me. No one can find me. I'm hiding from my kids. I'm de-stressing. I'm leaning against the inside walls. It is calm and dimly lit by shafts of sunlight coming down from up above me. It is a pleasant place to be. I am surrounded by my Lord. He tells me that I'm doing really well. He tells me to turn it over to Him. Peace envelops me. Just for a few moments. My Lord tells me again that He is pleased with me and it's ok. A small voice I know is His says:

"Let's go outside and do this together, shall we?"

When I leave the tower I know He will walk beside me because obviously I will have to come back to the real world and do whatever I'm needed to do but Jesus will strengthen me to the task.

3) And finally, the third verse is what I say as I climb upstairs:

Philippians 4:13:

I can do all things through Christ who strengthens me.

Sometimes I walk slowly up the stairs saying this verse feeling calm and ready and knowing I have a few extra centimetres of wick in my patience candle.

Sometimes I stomp up the stairs and say it fast, like a tongue twister, through gritted teeth really needing some kind of Holy Spirit zap of instant patience on my way up to see the kids.

Do you remember my candle analogy at the start of this topic? Without Jesus' help my candle of limited patience will burn out long before the day is over and I'll create a habit of being grumpy and irritated with my family in the evenings.

Interestingly, we are called to be both salt and light to the world. I found out recently that if you sprinkle table salt onto a burning candle it will burn down far more slowly. That fits this message so well. Add Jesus, like salt, to our light and it's a winning combination.

With His help I have the ability to endure far longer than I could in my own strength and I can make it through the day. I might even be good company for my husband in the few child-free hours we spend together in front of the TV once the children are in bed.

As I said earlier, I am still very much a work in progress when it comes to practising patience and I'm human – I don't always choose to lean on Jesus. When I do decide to ask for His help these are my go-to three verses. They are powerful, short enough to memorise and I can fall back on them when I need to. As I head through today towards another children's bedtime, I'll imagine my candle of patience burning long past its natural capability with His help. You can do the same.

When your patience runs out, take a moment to press your internal Pause button, speak God's Word and let His strength flood in.

 Prayer

Heavenly Father,

Thank You that You love me even when I get frustrated with my kids and let that frustration take over. I know I get cross. I over-react, shout and even sulk occasionally. I'm sorry for letting things get the better of me.

Thank You that You forgive me when I say sorry. Thank You that You know I am a work in progress just like everyone else. Help me to do better. I can't do this on my own.

When the little irritations of the day build up one after another and I start to feel myself getting wound up inside, please remind me to come to You.

When being a mum and looking after my children's needs feels like a heavy burden and the next straw will break my back, please help me to press Pause.

Please help me to use Your words in the heat of the moment, not mine.

I know Your words have power in them to make a difference. Help me to remember them, even if it's not quite right to start with.

Lord, please be my tower of refuge. Please walk with me and be my shield. Please work in me and give me more patience than I could ever have on my own.

In Jesus' name I ask.

Thank you, Lord,

Amen

 Recommended song

"This Is The Stuff" by Francesca Battistelli

Written by: Tony Wood, Ian Eskelin, Francesca Battistelli

Oh, do please listen to this song. It will make you laugh. It certainly made me laugh. It is full of up-tempo fun and perfectly describes a Christian woman at the end of her tether as her frustrating day doesn't go to plan. Granted, the lyrics are not small-child specific but I highly recommend playing it loud and singing along like no one is listening. I hope it will help you to see the funny side, regain your perspective and hand it all over to Him. Enjoy!

Mum Memories

Suggestion

Your space to use as you choose.

I'm sure you don't need any suggestions from me here. Probably what you need is a few extra blank pages!

Starting School Section

Starting school is "a thing" just like giving birth is "a thing". As the date of your child's first day at school gets closer, the more it occupies your mind and dark clouds can start to form.

For those of you who are about to watch your first little one walk into full-time education this can be an especially hard pull on the heart strings. Neither you nor your child knows what to expect and you are both learning as you go. All you do know is that visiting baby and toddler groups will no longer be possible and there will probably be no more cheap holidays outside of term time.

Equally, for those parents who are preparing for their youngest child to start school it marks the end of an era. It's as though the doors to the pre-schooler world are closing as you prepare to move on to school. Possibly your littlest is following older siblings into primary school and beyond. For all parents it marks the end of one chapter and the start of another.

It can be easy to follow the crowd and become downcast in the face of the inevitable, but the Starting School section is written to help you apply your faith in this changing season and go against the flow. It is written to hold your hand as you hold the hand of your little one, and enable you to smile and support them as they embark upon their big school adventure.

Of course, there are also necessary skills to master before school starts, such as toilet training, and we usually have to dig deep to travel through this particular valley. The Starting School section has words of encouragement as you guide your child away from nappies and towards the bathroom.

I share from my less-than-shining moments to let you know you are not alone, and throughout the focus is on gathering Bible-based comfort and strength so you can keep smiling and reassuring your pre-schooler as school approaches.

By now it will come as no surprise to know there is a song to accompany each topic. I do hope you find the time to listen to them. God uses music to uplift us when we need to stir up our hope, to boost us when we need an injection of faith energy and to make us smile when our sense of humour is on the edge of failing. Again, the lyrics are such a good fit, I really hope you enjoy them.

For the final time in this book – here is a summary of the topics covered and the recommended songs:

Toilet Training, Buttons and Zips

Recommended song
"When The Crazy Kicks In" by Francesca Battistelli

Staying In The Present Moment

Recommended song

"As Good As It Gets" by Francesca Battistelli

First Day At School

Recommended song

"Find Your Wings" by Mark Harris

The Starting School Intro video awaits you here if you would like to see it. Please scan the QR code or follow the link

https://mumschat.thinkific.com/courses/starting-school

Toilet Training, Buttons and Zips

Across the world children start school at different ages. Here in the UK children are 4 years old but in Spain they start at just 3.

In Poland and Finland children go to kindergarten from an early age but formal schooling begins at the age of 7.

For those of us whose little ones really are very little when school age arrives toilet training is a key part of making sure they are personally prepared to care for themselves in a school environment.

In fact, schools here in the UK won't take children unless they are toilet trained and I completely understand why that is the case. That's not to say they don't expect and prepare for the occasional accident.

My experience of toilet training my two children was radically different one from the other. My daughter was ready at the age of 2, and literally 6 weeks after her second birthday a potty was the must-have item in our house, in our car and in the shopping net of the buggy.

She was quick to learn (though of course there were occasional mishaps) but by the age of 2 years 6 months she was into the prettiest, tiniest princess underwear with matching vests – so cute.

My son, like most boys, was far too busy playing with his toys to show any interest in this area until he was 4. It's a good thing he is starting school aged 4 years and 11 months because he needed time to be ready, and now he sure is.

My point is that children are individuals, just like us adults, and although some generalisations can be applied, they will cross this particular bridge when they are ready. I estimated I must have changed about 3,650 more nappies for Daniel than I did for Ania but that's just the way it goes. Both scenarios were normal in terms of child development.

I bought a fabulous book on toilet training for boys when I decided that I wanted to toilet train Daniel. It had advice for parents, a reward chart with train stickers for my child and explanations of the best way to approach the topic. But my son just wasn't interested, and I had to shelve the whole idea for 6 months.

The main take-out of the book for me was that parents need bucket loads of patience and recognising when your child isn't ready is just as important as seeing the job through when they are ready.

Toilet training is yet another milestone along the way to independence for our children. It's a time when we really need our sense of humour, grace and patience, not forgetting a portable potty, several extra sets of clothes, toilet roll, nappy sacks and something suitable to carry things back home if doesn't go to plan when you are on the move.

Toilet training at home is one thing (at least you have everything to hand if accidents happen) but toilet training when you are out and about can be really challenging, especially if you've forgotten the potty pack. For most of us mums using public toilets with our little ones is filled with flash points and opportunities for something to go wrong.

First you get the announcement, "Mummy! I need to go . . . now!"

And you drop whatever you are doing, hold hands and rush to the nearest facility praying its available and that you get there in time.

You arrive and check the toilet seat has been left clean saying a short prayer of thanks if it has because every second counts.

You lift your little person onto the seat and hold them in position to stop them falling in because balancing on the edge is tricky to start with.

Then you both relax while they "perform" as my grandmother used to say.

Their "performance" is usually accompanied by an animated chat about truly random subjects.

Then a long strip of toilet paper is scrunched into a large ball and used in a way that leaves you suspicious that a thorough clean-up job has not been done.

And then, before you can check, off they happily jump.

If you decide to use this opportunity to "perform" yourself then the number of potential flashpoints doubles.

You know the scenario. While you are occupied your little one is magnetically drawn to the bin for sanitary waste.

"Don't touch!" you cry.

So, your child decides they are in for a really long, boring wait and they try to sit on the floor, which in a public toilet is usually not the cleanest place.

"Don't sit on the floor!" you say.

So, they decide to investigate the toilet brush.

"No! No! Leave that alone please!" you insist.

By now they are thoroughly bored and want to leave and start trying to unlock the door.

"Please wait until I'm ready to go!" you implore, hurrying up as you realise your dignity hangs in the balance.

Then when you are ready to go you need to remember to ask if they want to flush or it could ruin their entire day.

Especially if it is a toilet with a magic sensor that you wave your hand in front of to activate.

And once you come out you need to lift them up to wash their hands and, of course, they usually get their hands, their sleeves and you wet too.

But you can't use the electric hand drier because the noise hurts their ears.

And then you are both ready to face the world again.

It's no wonder we mums can get exasperated by the toilet-training experience – even when it goes well!

There are a couple of proverbs that come to mind for this testing time. You've probably heard of them. Obviously

Proverbs 22:6 (NKJV):

> Train up a child in the way he should go, and when he is old he will not depart from it.

I think this is probably meant more in relation to a child's spiritual training but it applies to toilet training too.

Another verse is Proverbs 16:32 (AMP), which says:

He who is slow to anger is better than the mighty, he who rules his [own] spirit than he who takes a city.

I imagine this verse is comparing controlling your own temper as being better (and possibly more difficult at times) than controlling an army of soldiers in battle.

Toilet training can be very testing indeed. Most little children have a phase when accidents just keep on happening and you wonder if you will actually run out of clean clothes.

I'm sure most parents have that really bad day when you wonder if you ought to go back to nappies. If you reach this point – please keep going. It is always blackest before the dawn.

All the toilet-training books tell us to stay calm and keep reassuring our little ones that everything is ok.

But in real life reassuring your little one that everything is ok and staying calm is not easy.

I remember being so infuriated with my son one day when we ran out of clean trousers that I was about as far from reassuring and calm as it's possible to get!

Once I'd gotten my frustration out of my system with a good old rant, Daniel looked up at me with big eyes and a sad, worried little face and said,

"Do you still love me, Mummy?"

Of course, I instantly melted and felt really bad for having gotten cross with him. I dropped down to his level and apologised to him and hugged him tight and told him it was all ok. We had a cuddle and found something clean for him to wear (it might have been a dressing-up costume) and he went back to playing with his toys.

I told myself privately, as I plodded yet again to the washing machine,

"We will get there. I can do all things through Christ who strengthens me."

Putting it into practice

There are a number of things you can do to help you through this process.

1) Enlist some moral support

Jesus sent His disciples out in twos because He knew they would each need someone to lean on at some point. This is no different. Is there a friend or family member who has parented their own children through toilet training? Someone you can trust to offer sympathy, support and encouragement without judgement? A listening ear and a kind word to help you stay the course? Even better if that person is someone who can pray with you too.

2) The practical potty pack

We've already looked at the practical aspects and the list of items I took everywhere I went (most of the time) during this learning phase. Your list might be different.

Perhaps it is longer or shorter. Perhaps you leave a bag permanently ready by the front door, so you don't spend time getting organised just before you leave. Trial and a lot of error meant I also left a mini back-up potty training pack in the car too, in case I left the house in a hurry. It usually included an old pair of kid's trousers that were a bit on the small side but in an emergency, we were all very glad of them.

3) Celebrating success

We've briefly touched on reward charts that can help motivate children to get on board with the endeavour. You can make these yourself if you want. I'm sure there will be ideas online to get you started. Celebrating success along the way is a really important part of the process for both of you.

4) Hurrah for hand-me-downs and charity shops

Stocking up on old clothes from a charity shop might be a good idea. My family and friends had given me lots of pass-me-down clothes in various conditions of wear and this was such a blessing. My children did not need to be wearing their best clothes as we pushed through toilet training. As long as we had something clean and sort of the right size, that was good enough.

5) A Bible verse to help you through

What can the Bible offer to help us through this challenge? I really like this verse in the Old Testament.

Proverbs 16:21 (AMP) says:

The wise in heart are called prudent, understanding and knowing, and winsome speech increases learning [in both speaker and listener].

"Winsome" doesn't mean you win some and you lose some. It's an Old English word that means kind and appropriate.

So, a wise toilet-training parent will be careful to show understanding and compassion and use winsome speech, i.e. kind, appropriate words tailored to the level of the listener so they can learn. And the parent who adopts this approach also learns because they see the result of their gentle approach brings progress towards the goal. Toilet training is one of those growing, stretching, learning phases that children have to pass through and we grow and stretch too.

I expect there will be times over the next few years when accidents happen. I still carry a potty and toilet roll in my car and I often still carry spare clothes and a disposable plastic bag in my handbag just in case. But with practice, encouragement and well-planned reminders, children learn when to "go and have a little try" before leaving the house, going to bed or travelling in the car.

Wherever you are in this particular phase please keep going. You are doing so well and you will both get through this.

Buttons and Zips

My son's future primary school also want children to be able to undress themselves out of school uniform and into their sports kit and then be able to change back into uniform again afterwards. Understandable, really, with 30 children in the class. So, just like toilet training, buttons and zips can become another pre-school milestone for our little ones.

Manual dexterity or fine motor skills are learned over time and with practice. Each skill helps towards mastering another and we all want our children to be able to hold a pen or a pencil for writing. At my son's nursery the classroom manager stitched a variety of round, colourful buttons onto a big piece of felt and gave it to the children to play with, one at a time. The game was to match the buttons to the colour-coded buttonholes on another large piece of felt and "do them up".

You might have something similar at home to teach fastening and unfastening buttons. The children at Daniel's nursery would sit down and practise till they got the hang of it and progress from the easier, big buttons down to smaller, more fiddly buttons when they were ready.

It's simple and genius at the same time because the children see it as play.

The children can grab a bean bag to sit down alone and quietly have a go or be supervised. Thankfully, this is a tool that you can make at home too.

Zips are another milestone for pre-schoolers and, if I'm honest, I'll admit that both my children learned this skill at nursery too. I think it was probably because of the number of times they went outside during the day to play and, due to our great British wet weather, each child usually had to put their coat on.

Putting it into practice

1) Proverbs in action

When I asked the nursery manager how she and her team had managed to teach 20 small children how to zip up their coats by the age of 3 she said:

"We show them first and we let them pull the fastened zip up on their own – which they love doing."

"And then we ask them to have a try themselves. They will have a go at all sorts of things at nursery because everyone else is having a go."

"And then whenever we play outside and put coats on we ask them to do their own zips. If they can't or they struggle, then we help them."

Practice, practice, practice all wrapped up in encouragement and help.

Isn't that Proverbs 16:21 in action?

The wise in heart are called prudent, understanding and knowing and winsome speech increases learning [in both speaker and listener].

2) Have a Plan B

If your child really struggles with buttons and zips then there's always that marvellous invention called Velcro! My son will need his school shoes to have Velcro fastenings for sure because tying up laces is a whole different level of challenge.

3) The Proverbs 31-woman vs our reality

Being kind to yourself is also a very important part of putting all of this into practice. In Proverbs 31:25-28 we read about a godly woman who seems to be going through the toilet training, buttons and zips phase of parenting and she is sailing through.

She rejoices over the future [the latter day or time to come, knowing that she and her family are in readiness for it]!

She opens her mouth in skilful and godly Wisdom, and on her tongue is the law of kindness [giving counsel and instruction].

She looks well to how things go in her household, and the bread of idleness (gossip, discontent, and self-pity) she will not eat.

Her children rise up and call her blessed.

It's all there, isn't it?

- preparing her family for the future
- kind words
- rejecting self-pity
- supported kids

It could have been written for this topic and this woman sounds amazing, doesn't she?

If I hold these verses up as a mirror to myself then I have to admit I find it difficult to be like her. I might do a good job on one aspect but fall down in another area. So, if this is you too then you are not alone. After an unexpected bed-wetting incident, I confess that I managed to give the encouraging words to my child (hurrah!) but I did then have a private pity party as I glumly carried the extra laundry downstairs (harrumph!).

And I lost count of how many times I got irritated as we tried to leave the house for church on Sunday morning and one of my kids insisted on doing up their coat zip on their own and they took ages and ages to do it but really wanted to try and we were already late and we'd miss a parking space and...Aaargh!

Sometimes, despite our best efforts and despite knowing Bible verses, we miss the mark and that's when we need to be kind to ourselves. We will need forgiveness from our family as we work through this stage because the process is stretching us too. Can you feel it?

Do be kind to yourself. Rather than using these verses above from Proverbs as a yardstick, against which I know I won't measure up, I look at these verses as a recipe containing the ingredients for a happy home with children who feel supported. Then I can put my energy into the areas needed in the moment rather than try to keep all the balls in the air at the same time.

At some point it might be saying kind words to my child. At another point it might be resisting the temptation to feel sorry for myself. One virtue at a time feels more manageable and realistic.

Toilet training, buttons and zips are important milestones for our little ones to master. They will get there and we will all be changed for the better once through to the other side.

Godly wisdom, kindness, giving gentle encouragement and instruction will get you and your child where you need to be . . . eventually.

And come the first day of school you will be the Proverbs 31-mother who rejoices over the future knowing that you and your family are in readiness for it. Little bit by little bit.

Keep calm, keep smiling, keep helping and be blessed x

 Prayer

Heavenly Father,

Thank You for this season. Thank You that my little one is growing and learning new skills. I know that You created us and You foresaw the need for toilet training of little children. Even Mary and Jesus had to go through this process together.

Please help me as I go through this challenge with my child because I am learning new skills too. At times I feel more stretched than ever trying to stay calm and give reassurance and encouragement. The cleaning-up process when things don't go to plan can be really unpleasant, so please harden me to this and help me through.

I pray for your blessing on my child to grasp these new skills, including buttons and zips. I pray for support for myself; show me who I can contact for an understanding, encouraging word. I pray for Your wisdom in the moment and peace of mind to know that we will get through.

In Jesus' name I pray,

Amen

Recommended song

"When The Crazy Kicks In" by Francesca Battistelli

Written by: Francesca Battistelli, Ian Eskelin, Tony Wood

Francesca Battistelli yet again brings us a song that conveys the reality of being a Christian mum. In the official video we see her juggling the demands of work with raising a young family and all the chaos that brings. She really understands. Although this is not toilet-training specific, she makes it clear how vital it is for her to grab just a moment at the start of her day to read her Bible and draw close to God and ground herself before it all goes haywire.

Our days when we are toilet training quickly go the same way and this really demonstrates the grab-it-and-go kind of faith that we are living out here. I chose this song for you partly because of the lyrics, which are so apt, but also because of the fun video and the uplifting melody. I hope it makes you smile and let's you know you are not alone. It might be a crazy time but Keep Going!

Mum Memories

Suggestion

Your space to use as you choose.

If you could design a Toilet Training Reward Chart for Parents, what would you put on it?

Staying In The Present Moment

Staying In The Present Moment can be a struggle, especially during the precious final year of pre-school. Many mums I've spoken with agree that, once you are in the last 12 months before your child starts school, your mindset changes and your heart can begin to ache. Starting school is on the horizon and as the year rolls through you advance far quicker than you would like towards your child's first day.

There can be a poignancy and a sadness that can tinge the happy days you spend with your pre-schooler. You know this is your last Autumn before they start school. You remind yourself that this is the last Winter before school. Suddenly you are in your last pre-school Spring and Summer with your little person and time is racing.

You may well see less of them once they are in full-time education Monday to Friday. You know there will be some adjustment and stretch coming for both you and your child. Knowing this special time is coming to an end can make you sad, feel under-prepared and just not ready.

There are usually some necessary practical actions for you to take to be ready, such as visiting primary schools and deciding which to apply to for a place. Then there can be a pause while you wait to see which school your child will be attending. Once you have this clarity you may need to buy a uniform, and all the time you will be readying your child for starting school and readying yourself to let go and allow them to take another step in their journey towards independence.

If your pre-schooler is your eldest then this last 12 months can be a worrying time for a mum. This whole "starting school" thing is new to both of you. You wonder how they will cope in a new routine and how the transition into school will play out. Questions might run through your mind such as:

- Did you choose the right school for your child?

- Will they make friends and be happy?

- Will they get a good teacher?

- How will the school run work in reality?

You might also wonder how you will cope and what this change means for you because this will be the first time you have been through the experience.

If your pre-schooler is your youngest child, then this last 12 months with your pre-schooler can be extra poignant. It means the end of the baby, toddler, pre-school phase of mothering. A season really is drawing to a close.

If you have worked part-time or as a stay-at-home mum up until now, then it's possible that visits to pre-school clubs and mother and toddler groups will stop. A whole support network that you might have found helpful will cease to be available.

If you have a job outside of the home, then dropping your child off at a trusted childminder or a nursery in which you have grown comfortable and confident will stop.

Regardless of how you have mothered your child up until now there will be a brand-new morning and afternoon routine for everyone around school drop-off and pick-up. Change looms.

Preparing yourself and steadying yourself as you move through this last 12 months is just as important as preparing and reassuring your child.

This *Mums Chat* topic is written in recognition that as a child heads towards starting school it can be an emotionally wobbly time for a mum.

Many mums will feel life is pulling them into a new phase that they always knew was coming but don't necessarily feel ready to embrace.

It is a letting go of a season that has been so special and has required you to give so much. And now you and your child are moving on but in different directions and this can feel tricky.

By the time your pre-schooler reaches his or her last 12 months before school their personality has emerged. They have good days and bad days. They are their own little person.

Many mums feel an anticipatory sense of loss as they realise their child will no longer need mummy quite as much. This little person is very slowly becoming more independent. I fully understand why many mums start to feel broody at this time – perhaps as a way to remain in this special season.

There is a 5-year-3-month gap between my daughter and my son. So, when Ania started school aged 4 she was my only child and I really did feel the seasons changing for me personally as I prepared us both for her to go to school.

During her first year in school I fell pregnant and now my son is about to start school, so again I'm feeling the baby, toddler, pre-school season coming to a close. And it is highly unlikely that I will have any more children at my age, so the pre-school season really is closing for me now.

I smile knowing that Daniel is ready to start school but at the same time I will miss him. Working part-time has enabled me to spend Mondays and Tuesdays with Daniel and he calls them "Mummy Days". Our routine on those days has involved going to pre-school clubs, playgroups and having occasional little café treats. All of this will change very soon. I will miss it all and I will miss Daniel in the same way that I missed Ania when she started school.

So, what can we do to steady ourselves in the months before starting school? How can we be positive when our heart is aching? How can the Bible help?

 Putting it into practice

Below are a few practical and Bible-based suggestions to help us mums as we walk towards this new phase of life feeling a little wobbly.

1) Focus on today – enter the present moment

Matthew 6:34 (AMP) has been so helpful to me:

> So do not worry or be anxious about tomorrow, for tomorrow will have worries and anxieties of its own. Sufficient for each day is its own trouble.

This verse tells us to focus on today and not allow fear, worry or dread to pull our focus into tomorrow or the future.

Today and now is all we really have and all we can really affect. Our joy is in the present moment. For me this came very much to life one Monday afternoon. Daniel and I had been to his pre-school football club. Imagine 12 tiny boys hurtling around an indoor sports hall chasing 12 small soccer balls for half an hour. Picture inevitable high-speed collisions and occasional disputes over which soccer ball is whose. Imagine 12 boys all volunteering to be the goalie at the same time. It's fun to watch and Daniel and I always go to a little café in our town afterwards to wait for primary school to end so we can collect Ania and then all drive home together.

Usually, I would read a newspaper and we would enjoy a smoothie each while Daniel played with the toys from the café toy basket. But on this occasion, I felt the pangs of sadness about Daniel starting school very keenly. How many more post-soccer café treats did we have left to enjoy? Maybe 15. Probably less.

I put the newspaper down and decided to join Daniel playing with the Lego blocks. I wanted to be fully present in his activity. He made a fabulous dinosaur about 40cms high.

We took photos with my phone. It felt good. The pangs of anticipatory sadness had lifted and gone. Entering fully into the present moment had resulted in creating a happy memory without a hint of sadness. I'd put all my focus on the present and the sadness about the future had gone. I'd switched my thoughts away from me feeling sorry for myself and instead forced my attention and my energy onto Daniel. And it lifted me.

I'm sure you'd agree that our pre-schoolers can teach us mums a thing or two about living in the present moment. They rarely understand about time and they really do live in the moment.

2) Get closure and celebrate how far you've come

The photo I took that afternoon of Daniel and his café building blocks dinosaur is very precious to me. It captures the joy of the moment and reminds me of that time in an instant. It is like a time capsule in a photo. It makes me smile. Daniel had enjoyed hooning around with his buddies, playing soccer and then enjoyed the building blocks. He was completely happy focusing on what was in front of him there and then and, when I joined him, so was I.

Maybe you can take a photo or find another way that captures the moment for you. Perhaps it is keeping an item of your child's clothing that evokes fond memories. You'll be so glad you did because you will look at it in the future and remember that time and see how far you've come since then.

3) Focus on the positives of the situation

Titus 2:11-14 (AMP) shows us mums the best way to approach this stage. It shows us to reject self-pity and gloomy thoughts and to avoid following others into wallowing in heartache. It says:

For the grace of God ...

has trained us to reject and renounce all ungodliness ... to live ... lives in this present world,

Awaiting . . . our Saviour Christ Jesus,

Who gave Himself on our behalf that He might redeem us . . . and purify for Himself a people . . . eager and enthusiastic about [living a life that is good and filled with] beneficial deeds.

It's all there, isn't it?

We are trained to reject sadness, dread and worry – which is the world's way of looking at this situation.

We are called to live lives in this present world. The word "present" in this scripture isn't an accident. Scripture calls us to live in the present moment and look for opportunities to enthusiastically do good deeds.

I think joining Daniel in building his dinosaur and taking a celebratory photo of it was an example of exactly that. He loved it when I stopped reading the paper and engaged in his activity with him.

4) Be a beacon of hope for other mums who are struggling

We are a people bought with Jesus' precious blood so that we can be free from all this gloom that the world associates with mums' hearts aching as children start school.

Instead, we are called to be eager and enthusiastic about living a life that is good and filled with beneficial deeds. And I'd take it one step further and say it's our opportunity as Christian mums to help others who are finding this time tricky. We can swim against the tide of sadness and uplift and encourage other mums who are struggling at this time. Help them to focus on the present moment, on the positives and enjoy every day as it comes.

1 Thessalonians 5:11, 16, 18 (AMP) say:

> Therefore encourage . . . one another and edify (strengthen and build up) one another, just as you are doing.

> Be happy [in your faith] and rejoice and be glad-hearted . . .

> Thank [God] in everything [no matter what the circumstances may be, be thankful and give thanks], for this is the will of God for you [who are] in Christ Jesus.

Try it. Go against the flow and help others do the same. Encourage other emotionally wobbly mums by telling them this is a good time. There will be plenty of long faces among the parents you know going through the same thing, especially those who don't know Jesus and the hope that He brings.

Be hopeful and joyful and confident in God's goodness and His ability to preserve you in this time. Be thankful for access to education because it is still not a given everywhere on the planet.

5) Be positive in what you say in front of your little one

Our little ones would far rather see us being calm and positive as school approaches both in our conversations with them and with others. They listen to everything we say, even if that conversation is way up above their head as we chat to another mum about starting school. So, for our children's sake, our words spoken on this topic in front of them need to be positive. It's a big step for our pre-schoolers. Far bigger for them than for us. A smile, a cuddle and an encouraging word will not only help your child, it will re-affirm you too.

And your consistency in this area, in every interaction, will bring hope and confidence for everyone around you.

Proverbs 18:21 (AMP) tells us that:

> Death and life are in the power of the tongue, and they who indulge in it shall eat the fruit of it [for death or life].

The words we speak are so important because they can activate God's favour and blessing in our lives or not.

If you can make the choice and choose to speak positive things about your child and yourself in regard to starting school this will help you to steady yourself and remain calm in the present moment.

I'm not suggesting denial.

Yes, you feel nervous, but you are also excited and expecting it to go well.

Yes, you will miss them, but they are ready for something new.

Yes, it will be a bit clunky getting into a new routine, but over time it will all iron itself out.

Yes, your mind does wander to thinking about it looming but you have some really effective techniques to help you come back to today again.

Now is all we can affect, and each moment is precious. Enjoy the time you have together before school starts.

Remember your child is going to school not the moon. You will still see them. Despite your misgivings they will still need you just as much as before but in gradually different ways.

6) Steady yourself by taking the focus off yourself

Remember, you will come through this. Focus on your child's needs rather than your own and lean on Jesus to see you through. What lies ahead is positive, exciting and necessary and it is still off and away in the future. I have chosen a song below that has steadied my heart many times and I recommend it to you. Finally,

Psalm 118:24 (NKJV) says

> This is the day the Lord has made; we will rejoice and be glad in it.

Be blessed as you spend time with your pre-schooler and enjoy the wonderful today.

 Prayer

Heavenly Father,

Thank You that You understand how it feels to say goodbye to Your child. You let Jesus leave heaven and come down to earth and I'm sure You missed Him. Father, I am going to miss the time I spend with my child once they are in full-time education. Thank You that You know how I am feeling as I get my little one ready to start school.

Saying goodbye, even for a school day, is hard. I keep thinking about that moment at the school gate on the first day. It is really looming for me and spoiling my remaining pre-school time. I need help to steady my heart.

As this final pre-school year unfolds, please help me to focus on the positives for my child. The excitement of advancing into full-time school. The making new friends. The learning new things and playing new games. Help me to be thankful that I live in a place where my child will receive an education. Help me to see that my child needs this change. It is a good thing. It is a blessing for both of us. Help me see the positives for me too.

Father, give me opportunities over the next few months to celebrate and get closure on this season. Help me to take some time to be fully in the present moment and feel the joy of it. I have come so far since my child was born. I have learned so much, given so much and received so much in return. Help my heart to know this isn't ending, just moving into another phase.

Thank You that You are always with me. You will never leave me. You hold my hand as I hold my little one's hand. We will do this together.

Thank you, Father,

Amen

 Recommended song

"As Good As It Gets" by Francesca Battistelli

Written by: Francesca Battistelli, Matt Maher, David Garcia

Oh, how wonderful is this song! Every word is carefully chosen and the melody is crafted with strings that reach inside and take me to another place. It is written like a story plotting childhood to adulthood and so it fits this topic very well for that purpose.

It also addresses the challenge of staying in the present moment when the world would pull us in different directions. Most importantly the chorus tells of putting Jesus in the centre of that quiet moment and focusing on Him and His all-enveloping love for us.

Time and again this song has enabled my heart to find stillness and peace and drawn me back into the present. It has been a blessing to me in many circumstances and I hope this song is a blessing to you too.

Mum Memories

Your space to use as you choose.

Suggestion

How can you cherish, capture and get closure on this season? Something simple and fun for both of you to enjoy together.

♥ ★ ❋

First Day at School

The first day of starting school is a "thing" just like the prospect of giving birth is a "thing". It's a life event that can fill a woman's mind as it draws closer. Starting school can be a source of anxiety and dread and sadness and grief for many mums (and dads). It is a very real letting go of one season and a moving on to a new season.

As has already been mentioned, this is especially the case if this is your first child starting school and so is a new experience for all of you. And it can be extra poignant if this is your youngest and final child to start school and pass through the pre-schooler years.

You become aware that you will have to learn new, different mothering skills to meet your growing child's needs.

As I write this *Mums Chat* topic, I am actually going through the starting-school process with my youngest and probably my last child Daniel. He has thoroughly enjoyed his time at nursery and learned so much more there than he would have at home with me.

You might remember that I mentioned in the previous topic that I have worked part-time during Daniel's pre-school years. I have spent Mondays and Tuesdays with Daniel, straight after the weekend, and he calls them "Mummy Days" because it's just the two of us together.

But this coming September he must start school. He will be one of the oldest in his class – turning 5 within the first term. He will really enjoy that.

On his first day I suspect he will be super excited to get up and put on his uniform. There will of course be the obligatory first-day photos for my husband and I to take with Daniel alongside his big sister Ania before they both set off to school.

I know his school will give him a gentle introduction with lots of playtime and toys and games to make the transition easier. I suspect I will pick him up and he will be happy but tired and perhaps a bit hungry. I also suspect that, by Friday morning of his first week, the novelty of going to school will have worn off a bit and he will not want to get out of bed.

It's possible he will say, "Can I have a 'Mummy Day' today?" and I'll need to explain that now he has to go to school like his older sister and try to coax him out of bed with a cuddle.

But how will I be on Day 1 and Week 1? How will you be? And what can the Bible offer us at this emotionally wobbly time?

 Putting it into practice

There are many things we can consider to get us through that first day, week, month of adjustment. A couple of these suggestions are repeated from Staying In The Present Moment, see if you can spot them.

1) Remember the tissues

This is a big day for both of you and it's ok to cry if you need to. Tears often fall down the cheeks of parents (mums and dads) on the first day of school. These may be:

- tears of pride in your little one's growing independence,

- tears of relief to have gotten your child this far and now be able to do something new for yourself or for others,

- tears of sadness as your heart aches to watch your little schoolboy or schoolgirl join their classmates and walk away from you through the playground and into class.

- And some parents may feel quite differently and won't cry at all as they wave their little one goodbye on their first day.

2) Focus on the positives of the situation

Picture the future in your mind's eye. Given that children have to stay in school until they are 16 years old in the UK I know this will be the start of 12 years of compulsory education

- of learning to read and write,

- of homework and school trips,

- the start of performing in school plays and making interesting models,

- the place where spellings and times tables will be learned by rote,

- the place where new friends will be found and possibly lost and then hopefully found again,

- certainly, it will be the place where items of school uniform are lost and never found again!

Daniel is ready and he needs this challenge. I am so grateful we live in a country where he can go to school. This is all good.

3) Support others

I want to support my son and I want to support other mums too. I encourage you to do the same. Take your focus off yourself and be a beacon of positivity in the playground. I will smile a big smile. I will walk with him as far as I'm allowed to go and then I will say to Daniel what I always say to Ania as we part in the morning:

> "Goodbye, God bless you and keep you safe. Go and have lots of fun. I'll be here to collect you later."

And then I will let my child go and let him grow and let him see me smiling and waving and cheering him on as he goes into class.

4) Make time for yourself

Once I'm out of the school grounds I imagine I'll walk quickly back to my car. Most probably my heart will be weighted down and I'll have a big lump in my throat but I'll still smile at the people I see as I go.

Maybe I will sit in my car and pray and cry for a bit. It's possible I will find it difficult to think straight that day and my mind may wander frequently to wondering what Daniel is doing and praying that he is having a happy day. This is all normal and I won't fight it. I'll get home and make a cup of tea and sit for a few minutes to gather myself and contemplate the points below.

5) Watch the season change

Do you remember what the Bible says about new seasons? I will remind myself that God created seasons in nature and the Bible refers to seasons in our physical lives and seasons in our spiritual lives too.

Ecclesiastes 3:1-2 (AMP) tells us:

> To everything there is a season, and a time for every matter or purpose under heaven:
>
> A time to be born and a time to die, a time to plant and a time to pluck up what is planted.

I love this imagery. A time to plant. My child will be planted like a tender young sapling into this school just like a gardener would carefully choose the best spot to nurture a healthy little infant tree.

Daniel's education will give him opportunities to take his life in whatever direction he chooses. His education will be both academic and spiritual.

Psalm 1:3 (AMP) also speaks of seasons and says:

> And he [or she] shall be like a tree firmly planted [and tended] by the streams of water, ready to bring forth its fruit in its season.

It is my prayer, and that of my husband Albert too, that our children both grow up to serve God and know and love Jesus. That they will each bring forth fruit in its season both in terms of what they choose to do professionally and how they progress God's kingdom while they are here on earth. School is just another step along the way to enable them to grow to maturity and be a blessing to others.

6) Embrace the "new"

As well as reminding myself that God created the seasons, I will remind myself that our God is a God of new things and fresh starts. And this certainly is a new start and a new thing.

Isaiah 43:19 (AMP) shows us how excited God was as He used His prophet to foretell the coming of Jesus.

> Behold, I am doing a new thing! Now it springs forth, do you not perceive and know it?

Psalm 33:3 (AMP) shows us how David enjoyed presenting God with new songs of worship.

> Sing to Him a new song; play skilfully . . . with a loud and joyful sound.

During his lifetime David was prolific in writing new psalm after new psalm. I'm sure God delights in hearing a new song just as much as we do. Staying put and doing the same thing over and over can lead to stagnation. We know very well that our pre-schoolers need something new to keep them engaged, usually every 10 minutes. They are curious and need variety in order to grow. In this context new is good. New is inevitable. Embrace the new.

7) Explore the personal opportunity

On that first day of school I'll also remind myself that there is a way through this for my own growth and development. My son is starting down a new road and so am I. I'm determined to choose a life-giving path as God advises in

Jeremiah 6:16 (AMP):

Thus says the Lord: Stand by the roads and look; and ask for the eternal paths, where the good, old way is; then walk in it, and you will find rest for your souls.

I really do feel as though I am at a crossroads now.

Like many mums at this juncture in life I want to go back to work Monday to Friday. How will I use that extra time? What work will God send my way?

This feels like an opportunity for me to stop and stand by the road and ask Him what is His will for my life now? Where is the eternal path that He has planned for me that I should take? I need to stop and ask and look and listen. I know I can trust Him to make my way clear. And I suppose the clue is in the scripture. If I choose the eternal path and I walk in it then it will give me rest for my soul.

8) Cast your cares

There is so much going on in our heads and hearts on the first day of school. It's a day with such mixed emotions. Pride and excitement for our little ones. Mixed in with tears that may or may not come (and either way – that's fine). Sadness and a heavy heart may be a part of it but it will lift over time. God is with us and He is faithful, and He cares very much about us.

1 Peter 5:7 (AMP) reassures us mums that we do the right thing in

Casting the whole of your care [all your anxieties, all your worries, all your concerns, once and for all] on Him, for He cares for you affectionately and cares about you watchfully.

9) Enjoy the reunion

However mixed up and fragile you are feeling – its ok. Be comforted, be reassured, you are all in His hands. School pick-up time will be here before you know it and your little one will be coming out of class and racing across the playground towards you with a big grin, possibly waving some new piece of artwork and very probably without their coat or their school bag. The new world of school is here.

If you can't be there at school pick-up then your reunion will be just as sweet when you get back from work. A smile, a great big cuddle, a "How did it go?" Before you know it, you will both be settled into a new routine and you will look back and praise God for watching over your parenting journey.

Smile, be brave and be blessed x

 Prayer

Heavenly Father,

Thank You so much for school and all the opportunities it brings for my child. The first day of school has arrived and I entrust my precious little one into Your care. Please send Your angels to guard, guide and keep him / her safe. Please send good friends for him / her to play and work with. Please let today be a happy day so tomorrow is easier. Please let this settling process go well for all the students and teachers.

Father, help me to find my own way through today and the days ahead. Let me see the positives and comfort me when my heart aches. Show me what is next in Your plan for me and help me to step into it.

I can look back at all the different challenges that early-years parenting has set before me and I know You helped me then and You will help me now. I trust You. I know You love us and have us in Your hands.

Thank you, Father,

Amen

 Recommended song

"Find Your Wings" by Mark Harris

Written by: Tony Webster Wood, Marcus R. Harris

I chose this song because it is performed by a loving dad who is singing a blessing over his child. It is perfect for this topic and the official YouTube video brings a lump to my throat every time. Parenting is walking a very long road of gradually watching our children grow and then letting them go completely and entrusting them to the care of our heavenly Father.

Mark sings with such feeling about the need to give his child the necessary freedom to find his own way in life but hopes his child will anchor himself in God as he seeks his path. As Christian parents, this is what we all hope for and this song captures that heartfelt desire perfectly.

Do get yourself a tissue before you download this track. If you are anything like me – you'll have that wonderful mixture of smiling through tears.

Mum Memories

Suggestion

Your space to use as you choose.

This space is possibly best left until you are a little way into school life. How has God already blessed both you and your little schoolboy / schoolgirl?

My Memory

Daniel came running out of school after his first day. He stopped in front of me with a big smile and pointed at his feet. There were tiny, blue metallic star stickers on the front of his new school shoes.

"I got twinkle toes for good behaviour!" he beamed.

Author's closing comments

Firstly, thank you very much for reading my book. I hope you found it encouraging and uplifting. I hope it has enabled you to see how your Christian faith, no matter how big or small you think it is, can help you when parenting gets tough, which it does quite frequently in the first few years.

I hope it has shown you that your heavenly Father longs for you to invite Him to be part of the journey and walk alongside you. I have a special Bible verse written out and stuck to the back of my kitchen door, next to photos of my kids, and it melts me whenever I read it:

Isaiah 30:18 (AMP):

> And therefore the Lord [earnestly] waits, [expecting, looking, and longing] to be gracious to you; and therefore He lifts Himself up, that He may have mercy on you and show loving-kindness to you.

This is your heavenly Father saying, "Please, let me help you." He is ever watchful, kind and loving. Letting Him join you in the highs and the lows of raising your children will be the best decision you can make in your parenting. I hope this book has given you some ideas as to how you can start or continue to do exactly that.

If you want to get in touch, please feel free. I don't "do" social media as it tends to "do" me instead. I wrote a poem about it that starts:

> *Nothing is greedier than social media*
> *"Your free time will be Mine, all Mine!"*

So, I prefer to keep my time to myself, hide my technological ineptitude from the world and give people other options for reaching out. My website is www.optimums.co.uk where you'll find a Contact page that pings your message through to my email. It would be lovely to hear from you and I'll get back to you as soon as I can.

 ## Final Recommended song

"The Blessing" by Kari Jobe and Cody Carnes

Written by: Christopher Joel Brown, Steven Furtick, Kari Jobe, Cody Carnes

This God-inspired song was written as the world went into Covid lockdown and, since 2020, it has been translated into so many different languages across the world. The original version is awesome, but I hope you will also find it online performed in your mother tongue.

It speaks God's blessing over you and your family in all that life brings and I cannot think of a better way to ask our heavenly Father to watch over you as we part.

Thank you very much, once again, for reading my book.

Blessings,

Marianne x

Acknowledgments

As the curtains close on this performance, will the following people please stand and take a bow . . .

Mums Chat was first issued at Little Angels, a church-based mother and baby group I was attending with Daniel in Malmesbury, Wiltshire. Back then each topic was a paper resource noisily churned out on my home printer. I have to thank the wonderful ladies at The King's Church, Abbey Row for their immediate willingness to let me leave my handouts for the mums attending Little Angels. If it wasn't for the encouragement of Barbara Eaton, Marie-Claire Davies and Sherry Baffour the entire *Mums Chat* concept would not have gotten far beyond my kitchen table. Thank you for giving me the chance to start bringing *Mums Chat* to other mums. Look what He has done with it since!

This book is based on the first 4 *Mums Chat* video series that I wrote, presented and produced in partnership with RightNow Media (yes, it is spelled like that) based in Texas, USA. Thanks need to go to the team there for believing in me as *Mums Chat* has grown to 6 series with another series planned for release soon. Paul Lanum and David Stidham, you have held my hand in the world of video publishing and this book wouldn't exist if you hadn't taken a chance on *Mums Chat*. Thank you for working with a rookie like me.

Equally, the 4 video series underpinning this book were filmed and produced with the help of a wonderful team that miraculously came together from nothing within the space of a week. Dave Bankhead, Frank and Leanne Punshon, Gemma Langdown, plus Gil and Elspeth Schwenk (RIP), you all played a significant part in *Mums Chat* and it was so much fun working with you. Thank you all.

Thanks also go to 2 pastors at Hope Church, Malmesbury, Lydia and Mark Faithful (such a great surname, hey!) for introducing me to RightNow Media's platform in the first place. Lydia and Mark, thank you for treating me as part of your flock, for your support with lapel mics during *Mums Chat* filming and supporting the Popcorn Preview nights of each *Mums Chat* video series as they launched. Thank you for your prayers over me and my work. I have always felt welcome within the Hope Church family and it is through Vicky, in your family, that I met Sarah Grace.

I never imagined the video series would be made into a book and for that I want to thank Sarah Grace and Malcolm Down at Malcolm Down Publishing who have shown me kindness and patience from the very start of the book-creating process. You opened a door I never expected would open and I am so grateful.

I also need to thank my publisher's elusive, anonymous "Editor" who has helped me to shape this book into something so much better than I ever thought possible. The Evaluation Report on manuscript 1 was brutal but brilliant. I have tried very hard to take your recommendations on board, all 5 pages of them. I think you are the publishing world's version of The Stig. Amazing!

I cannot express how delighted I am to see this manuscript transformed from a Word document into such a fun and friendly book. Sincere thanks go to Frank Punshon for the *Mums Chat* book cover artwork and, also to Angela Selfe for the Mums Chat interior book design. I will smile every time I hold it and open it.

I want to thank the amazing artists whose songs are recommended after each topic in the book. Your work has blessed me in so many ways through the darkest of times. Francesca Battistelli deserves a special mention. Thank you for writing songs that rend the heart but also lift the spirit. You have consistently captured a mother's voice in so many of the songs you have written. I hope, if you ever read this book, it makes you smile. I'll put a copy in the post and pray it reaches you.

Writing a book is not an easy process but two mums in particular have provided me with support and encouragement that made a huge difference in the gruelling re-writing process. Ali Avery in Hampshire and Fiona Simpkin in Wiltshire – thank you both so much for reading my revised manuscript and giving me your comments. I have no idea how you both managed to read anything at all over the Christmas holidays with your kids at home, but your feedback has helped me to push through to the end and hit my infeasibly tight self-imposed publishing deadlines. I owe you both. Something cold and bubbly will be opened when I see you next.

Behind this book are so many friends who have cheered for me, prayed with me, watched pilot videos and given me their feedback as the *Mums Chat* collection grew. Thank you to Tessa MacCallum, Fiona Simpkin, Kathryn

Bond, Glenda Navarro, Vicky Blackman, Nadine Benn, Cristina Trilla, Emma Walker, Monika Purcel, Sue Newton, Chantal Bryan OBE, Caroline Tye, Liz Glass, Lisa Derbyshire, Katherine Bailes and Meshel Bussey. There are many others and you know who you are. Your time investment, support and kindness has spurred me on.

Thanks to all at my mum's church, New Life Church in Cardigan, for your prayers and support. I appreciate you all so much. You are a godly powerhouse.

Thanks to Joel Sales, Kath Sales, Kaf Smith and Tom Morgan at wonderful Pattern Church in Swindon for welcoming us and making the growing of our family faith on Sundays so much fun. I look forward to seeing how God multiplies what you have started and being used in support.

Thank you to my mum, Kath Unsworth. I cannot express how your influence in my life, your unstinting prayer support and your faithful example of Christianity lived out day-by-day has not only helped make this book possible, but also helped me to become who I am.

Thanks also to my dad, Roy Unsworth, who's hides an excellent hymn-singing voice. Dad, your example of going to church alone as a boy and completing your Anglican confirmation programme, without any parental support, is an inspiration to me.

Nearly last, but certainly not least, I send a heartfelt *muchas graçias* to my own Fernandez family. Becoming a wife and mum has brought me immense highs and lows and I would not change anything. Thank you for being a blessing to me each and every day. To my husband, Albert, a special thank you for supporting me as I have followed God's call in a direction neither of us anticipated. Albert, Ania and Daniel, I love you all dearly.

Finally, I thank God, my heavenly Father, for the opportunity He has given me to share how much He loves us and our kids. He knows parenting is tough at times. There are so many challenges in the early years and this book captures but a few.

Heavenly Father,

Thank You for working in me and through me and for me. I am so grateful for all You have done and continue to do with *Mums Chat*. As I type the final words for this book, I put this work into Your hands. Please take this book where You will, to comfort, encourage and uplift mums around the world.

All the glory be to You.

In Jesus' name I ask,

Amen

More from Mums Chat . . .

Healing the Hidden Hurt of Miscarriage

The loss of a baby during pregnancy is a pain like no other. The world around you keeps turning and others think you've "gotten over it" but you know that you haven't. Mothers and fathers both mourn their loss, often in silence. This *Mums Chat* video series offers much needed tangible help that you can access when you are ready. Created to bring more than sympathy and comfort to grieving parents; the content gently guides you on a journey through your loss, explaining common emotions and thoughts during this incredibly difficult time. Drawing close to God throughout and sharing deeply from her own miscarriage experience, Marianne has created this series to offer you a way to validate your loss, access God's healing and give you hope for the future. Designed for use both privately at home or in small groups (including virtual groups) this *Mums Chat* series is available for you, and for others you know who would benefit. Subscription charge of £14.99 for 24 months unlimited access.

Scan the QR code below or follow the link to watch the free intro video to *Healing the Hidden Hurt of Miscarriage*.

https://mumschat.thinkific.com/courses/
healing-the-hidden-hurt-of-miscarriage

The Animals of Eden Valley

Who Made God?

ISBN 978-1912863-99-0

Join Roar and his friends as they explore the most popular kid's question of all time and looks at what the Bible says.

Scan the QR code below for more details
and to order use code **AUTH20** at the checkout
to claim **20% discount**.

The Animals of Eden Valley

Why Can't I See God?

ISBN 9781-915046-29-1

Join Roar and his friends as they explore the most popular kid's question of all time and looks at what the Bible says.

Scan the QR code below for more details and to order use code **AUTH20** at the checkout to claim **20% discount**.